A Century of Progress in the Aquatennial City

1856·1956

Minneapolis, CITY OF OPPORTUNITY

A Century of Progress in the Aquatennial City

Official Commemorative Book sponsored by

The Minneapolis Aquatennial Association

and The Minneapolis Centennial Committee

PUBLISHERS

T. S. DENISON AND COMPANY . MINNEAPOLIS, MINNESOTA

© 1956 by

T. S. DENISON & COMPANY

Printed in the U. S. A.

By The Brings Press   17

Library of Congress Catalog Card Number: 56-9982

Illustrations by Will Schaeffer

FOREWORD

Not every generation lives through a centennial and it is fitting
that we who do should leave a record for those who come after us.
This book is not intended as a formal history; it has been
designed solely to commemorate the Minneapolis Centennial.
We have attempted, however, to sketch in words and pictures
something of the color and romance, the vivid personalities and
the growth of business, industry, government, education and
the arts that have marked the city's story.

The growth of Minneapolis and the growth of industry have
been largely simultaneous processes; it seemed appropriate,
therefore, to invite a number of outstanding Minneapolis
businesses to share in the sponsorship of this volume. The response
was immediate and generous. It made this publication possible.

We hope you now hold in your hands a volume you will want to
keep through the years. The Minneapolis story is worth
remembering. If this book helps you, the reader, to that end it will
have served its purpose and justified the labors of the many
persons who participated in its production.

> Lawrence M. Brings, Editor-in-Chief
> Jay Edgerton, Editorial Director
> Edmund Kopietz, Art Director

THE PAST IS

One hundred year birthday parties, like other birthdays, can be times of unfruitful retrospection. Especially if we look back too long or too intently. We can mesmerize ourselves with our own pasts. But we need not do so. Wisdom, courage and imagination — to look forward to the next one hundred years — can save us from the merely memorial.

In the long view of human history, 100 years is a relatively short time. Minneapolis is a young city. Compared to London, Rome or Paris, our duration is scarcely worth notice. But time has various values. It differs from age to age. Some centuries are tremendously vital, dynamic growing times in the human story. Mankind seems to burst at the seams of time.

Consider Minneapolis' own first century. When the city was born, an outpost on the far-flung American frontier, Abraham Lincoln was a country lawyer. Gold had been dis-

PROLOGUE....

covered in California less than 10 years before. The Civil War was still five years away in the future. The first transcontinental railroads remained to be built. West of the Mississippi, wild Indians roamed buffalo plains that had never known a plow.

Our century, Minneapolis' first 100 years, has been one of the great transforming times of man's history. It has been a time of yeasty ferment, of startling growth and development, of far-reaching, influential conquests in science, industry, medicine, art and government. In this brief, crowded ten decades man has moved from the horse-drawn plow and the river steamboat to the jet airliner and the atom-powered engine.

Minneapolis reflects the century of its birth in many ways. From the beginning, it has been brisk, enterprising, on the move and forward-looking. One hundred years ago Sioux tepees stood on the site of Bridge Square. Today, Bridge Square and all the surrounding country are covered by one of the great cities of America — a city of tens of thousands of fine homes, of towering office buildings and beautiful stores, of great flour mills and productive factories, of parks and churches, schools and colleges.

Through all its 100 years Minneapolis has been a dynamic city. It never has stood still. That's one of the reasons its story is worth telling. Our century has been a beginning, a kind of first chapter in a book that is still being written. In a very real sense we can discern the face of tomorrow in the glass of yesterday. We can say of Minneapolis on its 100th birthday what is carved in stone on the National Archives building in Washington — What's Past is Prologue.

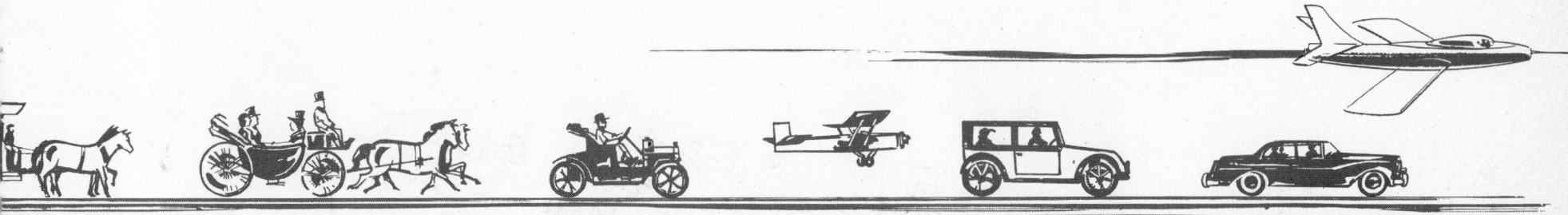

FLAGS FOLLOWED

For men of the mid-Twentieth century, concerned with electronics, uranium and atomic fission, it is difficult to understand the intensity with which their forebears pursued the beaver. Not gold, not diamonds, not rubies have been sought more eagerly — nor with greater cunning, avarice and cruelty. In the Eighteenth Century beaver was king.

The beaver's soft, luxurious pelt was coveted by the noble ladies and lordly gentlemen of Europe's courts. By a thousand waterways, great and small, the hard, wild adventurers of France, Spain, Great Britain — and later the United States — pursued him to satisfy these wants and to reap the reward. In less than a century the place we now call Minneapolis flew four flags.

Down to the middle of the Eighteenth Century, France reigned supreme in mid-America. French canoes plied the western lakes and rivers, carrying back to Montreal, Quebec and Trois Riviére rich cargoes for the fur-hungry nobles and

THE BEAVER

wealthy burghers of Europe. French songs rang above the western waters and in a thousand far-flung Indian lodges Frenchmen mingled their blood with the native tribes.

But the Eighteenth Century was a century of conflict. The prize: the North American Continent. By 1759 the English had emerged victorious. Wolfe had defeated Montcalm on the Plains of Abraham and the Fleur-de-Lys had fluttered down forever from the battlements of Quebec.

By the peace treaties of 1763 the country east of the Mississippi River, which would include southeast and northeast Minneapolis and all the old village of St. Anthony, came under British sovereignty. France had already ceded the country west of the river to Spain in the treaty of Fontainebleau in 1762. Down to a short time before the Louisiana Purchase in 1803 the western country remained Spanish.

With the coming of the American revolution, the flag on the east bank of the Mississippi changed again. Twenty years later both sides of the river were United States terri-

tory. Thus, in the century following Father Hennepin's discovery, the land on which Minneapolis stands had been under the flags of France, Spain, Great Britain and the United States.

Since the Revolution, Minneapolis land or parts of it have been under eleven different American jurisdictions. In the early days Virginia claimed the east bank. Later, east Minneapolis was part of the territories of Indiana, Illinois, Michigan and Wisconsin. The west bank was held by the territories of Louisiana, Missouri, Michigan, Wisconsin and Iowa. And, of course, both sides were and are Minnesota.

Within a few decades of the coming of Americans, the dress and living habits of Europeans changed. Settlement drove out the fur hunters and their quarry. The fur trade declined. Beaver was no longer a furry gold mine. But for two centuries, through exploration, war and conquest the flags of many nations had followed him.

ST. ANTHONY FALLS - - -

Father Hennepin

This map appeared in Father Hennepin's book "A Description of Louisiana" published in 1683. The legend reads: "Map of New France and Louisiana newly discovered. Dedicated to the King in the year 1683 by the Reverend Father Louis Hennepin, Recollect Missionary and Notary Apostolic."

In the Seventeenth Century the French were pushing westward from the St. Lawrence valley along the network of mysterious and beckoning waterways that led to the heart of the North American continent. Men dreamed of a water passage to Cathay. Eventually, the dream faded into the golden reality of the fur trade.

Many French names are written on the Minnesota land— Groseilliers and Radisson, Du Luth and Le Sueur, to name only a few — but in the history of Minneapolis one takes precedence over all, Father Louis Hennepin, the Belgian Franciscan, who named St. Anthony Falls.

Some of the facts of Father Hennepin's life are obscure. It is uncertain when or where he died. He was baptized April 7, 1640, at Ath in the province of Hainaut, Belgium, then a possession of the Spanish crown. He entered the Recollect Franciscan order probably in 1660 and was ordained a priest about 1666. In 1675 he came out to New France (Canada) as a missionary and by 1680 he was in the western country with LaSalle.

Today most of us take St. Anthony Falls for granted. But in the seventeenth and eighteenth centuries they were a great landmark at the continent's heart. This was an age when men needed landmarks. They were pushing, every year, deeper and deeper into unknown and perilous country. After 1680,

Landmark at the Continent's Heart

Father Hennepin's discovery stood as a marker on the western water trails.

Father Hennepin and two lay companions left LaSalle's fort in the Illinois country on the last day of February, 1680. LaSalle wanted a report on the upper Mississippi river country. Early in April, Father Hennepin and his party ran into Sioux raiders descending the river. The Sioux took them upstream, through Lake Pepin, and probably as far north as St. Paul, where the party struck overland to the big Sioux encampments around Mille Lacs.

The missionary and his companions remained with the Indians, virtual prisoners, until mid-summer, when the Sioux left for their yearly buffalo hunt. Father Hennepin was allowed to depart. He paddled down river in the hope of finding Frenchmen and supplies on the Wisconsin. It was on this journey that he found and named St. Anthony Falls — for St. Anthony of Padua, the patron saint of his own native Franciscan province in France.

From that day on St. Anthony Falls was a beacon of western travel. Within a few years, its name appeared on all the maps, inaccurate though these were. Voyageurs, the far-ranging men of the fur trade, calculated distances to and from the falls. The Indians had called the falls a dwelling place of gods. White men immediately recognized their significance and their importance.

Capt: JONATHAN CARVER.

The Captain From New England

Ten years before the American Revolution, a Massachusetts militia captain who had served with distinction in the French and Indian War stood at the foot of St. Anthony Falls and was amazed.

"They fall perpendicularly about thirty feet," he wrote in a famous book published twelve years later, "and the rapids below, in the space of 300 yards more, render the descent considerably greater; so that when viewed at a distance they appear to be much higher than they really are... In the middle of the Falls stands a small island, about forty feet broad and somewhat longer, on which grow a few cragged hemlock and spruce trees... The country around them is extremely beautiful..."

The captain was Jonathan Carver, asso-ciate of Robert (Northwest Passage) Rogers and the first Englishman to publish an account of St. Anthony Falls. The book was "Travels through the Interior Parts of North-America, in the Years 1766, 1767, and 1768." It was a best seller in its time.

Carver died in poverty in England in 1780. After his death claims were made that Sioux chiefs had deeded him land from St. Anthony Falls to the south end of Lake Pepin and stretching 100 miles eastward from the Mississippi. For many years so-called "Carver heirs" besieged Congress, and later Minnesota governors, with claims. Nothing ever came of them. It was doubtful the Sioux ever had the chiefs named in the "deed." In any event, there could have been no valid transfer of land.

Lt. Zebulon M. Pike

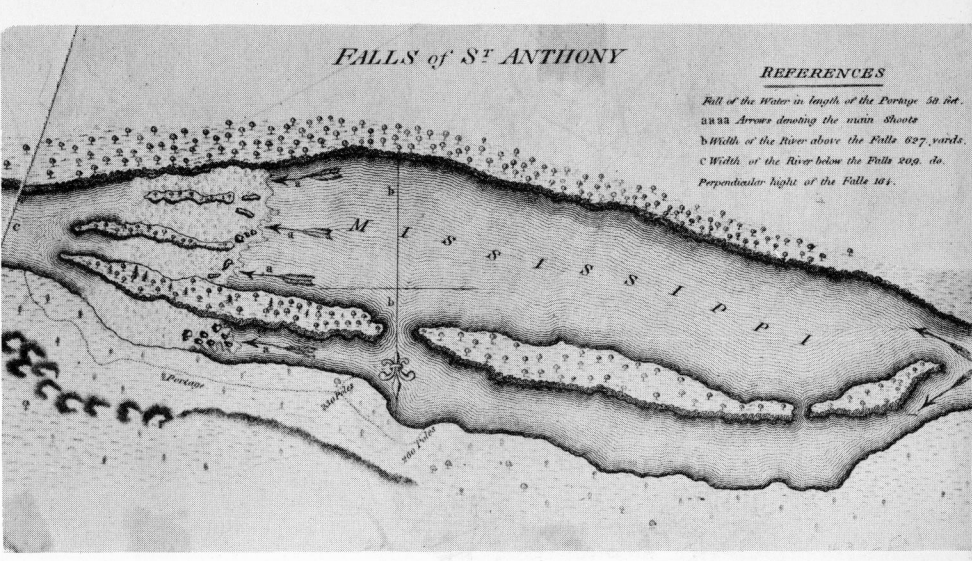

FALLS of St ANTHONY

"You Will Obtain ...
THE FALLS OF ST. ANTHONY"

On July 30, 1805, the American officer commanding at St. Louis, General James Wilkinson, issued orders to a twenty-six-year-old lieutenant who was to leave his name on one of the most famous mountain peaks in the world — Zebulon Montgomery Pike.

"You will be pleased to obtain permission from the Indians who claim the ground, for the erection of military posts and trading houses, at the mouth of the river St. Pierre (the old French name for the Minnesota river), the Falls of St. Anthony, and every other critical point which may fall under your observation," the General wrote.

In compliance with these orders, young Lieutenant Pike, a sergeant, two corporals and seventeen privates came up the river in a 70-foot keel-boat in August and September, 1805. And on September 23, at noon, Pike met in council at the mouth of the Minnesota River with Little Crow, one of the Sioux chiefs, grandfather of the Little Crow who lead the Uprising of 1862. Here was signed the first conveyance of land in Minnesota. It included a large portion of the site of modern Minneapolis.

The price paid was about 1¼ cents an acre.

Chief Little Crow signed over land extending nine miles on each side of the river from the Minnesota up to and including St. Anthony Falls. He also sold an area nine miles square at the mouth of the St. Croix.

From his big real estate deal, the young lieutenant Pike went on into fame and history. He explored the sources of the Arkansas and other southwestern rivers, was taken prisoner by the Spanish, promoted to major, colonel and then brigadier-general. He was killed in the War of 1812.

13

Where the rivers meet . . .
A FORT

Major Stephen H. Long

The War of 1812 taught the young United States some hard lessons. One was that the northwest frontier, whatever it might be legally or by international treaty, was in point of fact British.

British traders ranged at will over the area. The Indians liked British goods and British traders and the Sioux were avowed British allies. At the siege of Detroit and on raids as far away as the Ohio valley, British officers led active and enthusiastic war parties from the Sioux of Minnesota.

Anyone who could read a map could see that a key point between the Great Lakes and the Missouri valley was the confluence of the Mississippi and the Minnesota rivers (then called the St. Peter's). Pike had seen it as early as 1805. In the summer of 1817 Major Stephen H. Long of the topographical engineers came up the Mississippi in a six-oared skiff and found the place where the rivers meet a good one for a fort.

"A military work of considerable magnitude might be constructed on the point." Major Long observed, "and might be rendered sufficiently secure by occupying the commanding height in the rear in a suitable manner, as the latter would control not only the point, but all the neighboring heights, to the full extent of a twelve pounder's range. The work on the point would be necessary to control the navigation of the two rivers."

By Christmas time of 1817, John C. Calhoun, then secretary of war, had convened a board of high officers to work out a frontier defense line for the young Republic. A year later it was announced in Washington that a fort would be constructed at the mouth of the Minnesota River.

Early in 1819 the Fifth Infantry was ordered to concentrate at Detroit under command of Lieutenant Colonel Henry Leavenworth. Leavenworth was directed to take his men by way of the Great Lakes to Fort Howard on Green Bay, thence by the Fox and Wisconsin rivers to Fort Crawford at Prairie du Chien on the Mississippi. From there, part of the command was to go up the Mississippi to build the fort at the mouth of the Minnesota, and part was to garrison Fort Armstrong at Rock Island. Headquarters of the divided regiment was

14

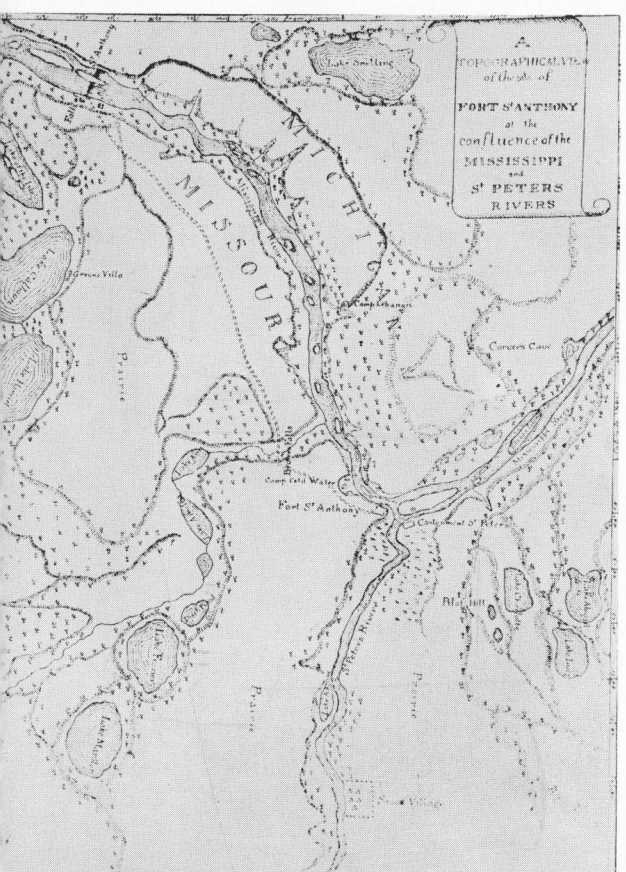

to be at the new post on the Minnesota.

The Leavenworth party set out from Prairie du Chien in early August, 1819. There were 98 soldiers and 20 boatmen in 17 boats of various sizes. The party included two women and a baby — Charlotte Ouisconsin Clark (Van Cleve), daughter of a regimental officer. The baby had been born an hour after the command had reached Fort Crawford.

By August 17 the troops were at the lower end of Lake Pepin and on August 24, Colonel Leavenworth's barge, ahead of the main body of troops, reached what we now call Mendota. Leavenworth spent the day looking over the ground and finally selected a campsite on the Mendota side of the river. When the troops arrived they lived on the boats until they had completed a series of huts and log cabins which was given the name of Cantonment New Hope. In September the little garrison was rein-

forced by 120 recruits from Prairie du Chien.

That first winter, 1819-20, was a bitter one. Scurvy, the dread killer of frontier outposts, (now classified as a deficiency disease caused by lack of Vitamin C), broke out in virulent form. Men went to bed at night never to wake again. At least forty soldiers died. Some estimates place the total casualties at almost half the command.

In the spring, Colonel Leavenworth decided to move across the river to the west bank of the Mississippi, somewhat north of where the old Round Tower stands. There was a spring here and the troops, living in tents, called the place Camp Coldwater.

And here, a year after their arrival, the men of the old Fifth received their second commander on the Minnesota frontier — a vigorous, dynamic, born-executive who was to leave his imprint on the region and the future city, Colonel Josiah Snelling.

15

THE COLONEL HAD RED HAIR

Boston-born Josiah Snelling, a red-haired man tending to baldness, was thirty-eight years old when, in the summer of 1820, he came up river to relieve Colonel Henry Leavenworth at the fledgling frontier outpost called Fort St. Anthony.

Snelling already had some reputation in the army. He was known as a worker and a disciplinarian. Sometimes he personally whipped insubordinate soldiers. He had entered the army as a first lieutenant of the Fourth Infantry in 1808. He commanded a company at the battle of Tippecanoe. At the surrender of Detroit in the War of 1812 he had distinguished himself by refusing any part in the raising of the white flag. He had emerged from the war a lieutenant colonel. On occasion he displayed a peppery temper. His men called him "The Prairie Hen."

Colonel Snelling disapproved Leavenworth's location of the new fort and moved it to the exact point of land between the Mississippi and Minnesota rivers. In the winter of 1820-21 soldiers were sent up to the Rum River to cut logs which were floated down to the Falls of St. Anthony in the spring. These were cut into lumber and hauled to the fort. By the fall of 1822 troops were moving into new barracks. In the summer of 1823 the soldiers were building an Indian council house.

In 1824 Fort St. Anthony received a famous visitor, General Winfield Scott, inspector general of the army, veteran of the War of 1812 and destined to be the only lieutenant-general between Washington and Grant. General Scott was pleased by what he saw — and pleased with the little post's commanding officer.

"I wish to suggest," he reported to Washington, "the propriety of calling this work Fort Snelling, as a just compliment to the meritorious officer under whom it has been erected."

By general order of January 7, 1824, the General's suggestion was accepted — and with that name, the name of the red-haired "Prairie Hen", Fort Snelling has passed into history.

16

The Gentleman From Virginia

Little Crow, A Sioux Chief. This Indian was chief of Kaposia village near South St. Paul. He was dressed in full regalia when this portrait was made by Frank Mayer in 1851. Little Crow led his people in a bloody uprising against the whites in 1862.

Some men become legends in their lifetimes — and sometimes the legends linger down the years. Such a man was the proud Virginian, Lawrence Taliaferro, friend of President James Monroe, Indian agent at Fort Snelling from 1819 to 1840. Even today out on the plains of the Dakotas, old Sioux — who had it from their fathers and grandfathers — speak with a strange light in their eyes of Lawrence Taliaferro.

"Major Tolliver", for so early Minnesotans called him, brought honor, courage and justice to a messy business — the Indian trade. And the Sioux never forgot him. He fought their battles with fur traders, whisky peddlers and army officers. Many times he dug down into his own pocket to feed hungry Indians.

After his retirement in 1840, his house in Washington was a port of call for all visiting Indian delegations. He foresaw and foretold the bloody Sioux Uprising of 1862. When Little Crow saved the lives of white women and children at Redwood, he remarked, "I spare the lives of some of you for the sake of our good old Father, Mah-sa-busca (Iron Cutter): his words are this day in my ears; had he been here this war would not have been."

Major Taliaferro re-entered the army in 1857 and was permanently retired in 1863. He died at 77 in Bedford, Pa., in 1871. He was Minneapolis' first practicing humanitarian.

17

Fort Snelling, located and established in 1819 where the Minnesota River joins the Mississippi, was the first permanent American occupation of Minnesota. The coming of Lieutenant Pike to the area, the building of the Fort and other early day incidents covering a period of forty years, are portrayed in the Richard Haines mural housed in the reconditioned Round Tower Museum (below at left) at Fort Snelling. At the right in an interior view showing a portion of the mural which is six feet high and 108 feet in length around the room.

Scenes depicting the building of Fort Snelling and the beginning of lumbering and the inauguration of American rule with the surrender of British flags and medals to Major Taliaferro.

Out of necessity, soldiers were stern and serious in keeping law and order. The military was also responsible for licensing fur traders as shown in these scenes above from the Haines mural.

Important and welcome events were the arrival of ox drawn carts from the Red River Country or the coming of the first steamboat, which reached Fort Snelling in 1823, eight days out of St. Louis. Here, too, the first church services were held, the first school taught in Minnesota.

"Across the Prairie to the Government Mill . . ."

Long before there was a city Americans made good use of St. Anthony Falls water power and for precisely the things that ultimately brought fame and fortune to Minneapolis — lumber and flour.

In its cold and hungry infancy the little army post nine miles down river needed lumber and flour — lumber to protect itself against the long northern winters — flour to feed its hungry garrison.

Colonel Josiah Snelling saw the means to satisfy both needs in the standing timber along the Rum River to the north, in the broad fertile prairies around the fort

and in the water power at St. Anthony Falls.

The first winter of Snelling's command a military party was sent north to cut trees. More than 2,000 logs were rafted down the Mississippi in the spring. Meanwhile a saw mill had been built at the falls. The logs were sawed and hauled to the fort by teams. The lumber was used not only for buildings but for most of the early furniture at the new army post.

By the spring of 1823 Colonel Snelling had wheat sown around the fort. He was forecasting a good crop. Up the river from St. Louis, at his requisition, came two dozen sickles and a pair of millstones. The latter went into the flour mill which, by this time, had been completed.

The mills became a little community at the falls. In addition to the two working buildings there was a house for the mill guard detachment. This varied in strength from time to time. There appear to have been years when only a sergeant was on guard. At other times a lieutenant with eight to ten men occupied the guardhouse.

Almost from the beginning "The Old Mill" was popular for outings and picnics. Officers from the Fort and their ladies took the nine-mile ride along the river to enjoy an outdooor meal at the falls. Travelers invariably stopped there. Looking back more than forty years, Stephen R. Riggs, the noted missionary to the Sioux, wrote in a nostalgic mood in 1880, of "a pleasant ride across the prairie to the government saw-mill" which he and his wife took in 1837.

The government ran the flour mill, off and on, down to 1849. That year the first term of court was held at the mill by Judge Bradley B. Meeker, associate justice of the supreme court of Minnesota Territory. The flour mill was sold in 1849 for $750 and the saw mill was leased in 1855. A few years later the flour mill was torn down but the saw mill was converted to grinding flour and continued in operation, privately, until 1879 when it was destroyed by fire. The building of the Northwestern Flour Mill in 1879 removed the last traces of the old government mills "across the prairie."

Godfrey's Mill in ruins.

Below, logs in plentiful supply.

21

A Frontier Love Story

Philander Prescott, the government farmer for the Indians at Lake Calhoun, was, in his younger years, one of those restless, ambitious youths so often found on the American frontier.

The son of an upstate New York doctor, Prescott left home at seventeen and headed west by way of the Great Lakes. He worked first for Mr. Devotion, sutler (army post storekeeper) at Detroit and Fort Snelling, and later entered the Indian trade.

Like many a trader, young Prescott had an eye for Indian girls and for one in particular, Mary, the daughter of old Kee-e-he-ie of the Lake Calhoun band. The father had run up a bill at Prescott's trading post and the young trader took the bright-eyed, straight-haired girl in settlement of account — not an unusual practice at this time on the frontier. They were married according to Indian custom.

Indian marriages were held lightly by men of the old West. Prescott was no exception. When the wanderlust struck again, he thought nothing of leaving Mary and his Indian children. Traders did it all the time. He headed south and west, expecting never

View of Fort Snelling by artist Seth Eastman, in the collection of the Minneapolis Institute of Arts.

job. Pack on back, he set out for the Missouri country. Through unbelievable hardship and privation, he tramped the unmarked prairies. And then one day he came over a rise to look down on the fugitive smoke of a Sioux teepee town.

Mary was surprised and delighted to see him. In the simple Indian way, she welcomed him back with no explanations demanded. She knew the old trader story well. It had happened to many Indian girls. This was too good to be true. So why talk about it? This was not enough for Prescott, however. He insisted they travel hundreds of miles to a missionary outpost to be married by an ordained minister of a Christian church.

Mary was baptized and so were the children. From 1837 to 1855 the Prescotts had a house near Fort Snelling. It became a favorite stopping place for frontier travelers. After the Sioux removal to the upper Minnesota River, Prescott and his wife and children moved out west to be with her people. In the Uprising of 1862, Prescott was warned of impending danger by Little Crow but failed to escape. A Sioux war party shot him down not far from Fort Ridgely.

Mary lived on until 1867. She died at the home of her son-in-law, Eli Pettijohn in Shakopee. She and Philander were buried side by side in the old Layman's Cemetery in Minneapolis.

to be bothered again with his Lake Calhoun family.

But somewhere far out on the upper reaches of the Sabine River in Texas what he thought afterwards was the hand of God reached out for him. Prescott stopped to listen in on the camp meetings of a frontier revivalist. Remorse and shame for his treatment of his Indian family swept over him.

Prescott headed back north, determined to find Mary and his children. He reached Fort Snelling only to learn that they had left with a Sioux band and probably were somewhere "out west" on a buffalo hunting trip near the Missouri.

To find a wandering Sioux hunting party in the uncharted regions beyond the Coteaus of the Missouri was task enough for the best scout. But Prescott was equal to the

The Brothers

P O N D

That shrewd man, Lawrence Taliaferro, knew that his Indians could not live by bread alone but he believed that agriculture and the arts should precede the teaching of the Gospel. By the 1830's he had the Lake Calhoun Sioux farming, and then, as if by dispensation of Providence, he received two strong instruments for carrying his plans a step further in raising the red man out of barbarism.

These were the brothers from Connecticut, Samuel William and Gideon Hollister Pond, 26 and 24 years old respectively, deeply dedicated young men moved by profound religious convictions to do something for the Indians. They were without ordination or authorization from any religious body, indeed even without permission to enter Indian country, when on May 6, 1834 they arrived on the river steamboat, Warrior, at Fort Snelling. They were immediately summoned by the commanding officer to explain their illegal entry of Indian territory.

Major Lawrence Taliaferro did posterity a real service by capturing on paper a graphic record of the Minneapolis-St. Paul area as it was in 1835. This primitive map provides a glimpse of the almost unsullied land as it looked before it was settled by the white man.

Samuel W. Pond

Gideon H. Pond

Fortunately for the Ponds — fortunately, too, for Minnesota and Minneapolis—there was work to be done. The frontier needed young men like the brothers from Connecticut. They were keen, friendly, lean and sinewy and both more than six feet tall. They had the jerked-buffalo-meat look of the Old West — and there was a job that needed immediate doing. Big Thunder, father of Little Crow, wanted plowing at Kaposia, the Indian village down river from Fort Snelling. Young Samuel Pond offered to give him a week's lessons.

Major Taliaferro liked the looks of the brothers — and he had just the place for them, Cloud Man's village at Lake Calhoun. There is an old story that Cloud Man himself selected the site for the Pond cabin on the east shore of Calhoun because, from it, the missionary brothers would be able to see the loons on the lake.

Major Taliaferro sent over axes, tools, oxen and a log chain from Fort Snelling. Ground was cleared. Slabs were brought from the government mill at St. Anthony Falls. By mid-summer the second white man's structure within the present city limits of Minneapolis was ready for oc-

cupancy, a snug two-room cabin of oak logs, twelve by sixteen feet and eight feet high. Total cash outlay: 12½ cents for nails.

One of the officers at Fort Snelling had been collecting Siouan words. With this as a start, the Brothers Pond went to work to master the Sioux tongue. By the time the cabin was completed they had devised what has passed into history as the "Pond alphabet" of Sioux. Shortly afterwards they taught one of the younger members of Cloud Man's band to read.

A year after the Ponds' arrival, in 1835, Rev. Thomas S. Williamson and Rev. Jedediah D. Stevens reached Fort Snelling. Williamson went on up the Minnesota to establish a mission at Lac qui Parle. Stevens moved out to the lakes. An Indian mission school was established on the northwest shore of Lake Harriet.

In the Sioux-Chippewa war of 1839 the Pond's cabin was torn down to provide materials for defensive works. The brothers moved back towards Fort Snelling where they remained until 1842. That year they established the mission at Oak Grove, eight miles up the Minnesota River from the fort.

25

9. The Dakota Friend. This shows the heading of a paper published in their own language for the Sioux, who were also called the Dakota Indians. Its editor was Gideon H. Pond, a missionary to the Sioux.

LAKE CALHOUN CHIEF . . .
Cloud Man and Eatonville.

Treaty of
Traverse des Sioux—

Painting by
Frank B. Mayer
Minnesota Historical
Society

As white men moved into the developing west some of them were concerned about the plight of the Indian. It was apparent that the old ways of the hunt and war path were doomed — and within a very few years. At Fort Snelling the Indian agent, Major Lawrence Taliaferro, gave long and deep thought to the problem. He believed the Indian should be taught to farm and to accept the ways of white men. He found an unexpected ally in Minneapolis' own Sioux chief—Marpiya-wichasta or Cloud Man of Lake Calhoun.

This Cloud Man, who had been born in a Sioux village on the Minnesota river probably in the last quarter of the Eighteenth Century, was a remarkable person for his time and place. Defying tribal conventions, he set his face against war early in life. "War begets war," he remarked. He was impervious to Indian taunts that he hoed corn with the women.

Some fine blood strain seems to have run through the Cloud Man family for his descendants became physicians, writers, clergymen and bankers. The Indian doctor-writer, Charles Eastman, Ohiyesa, a graduate of Dartmouth, was one of his great grandsons.

26

The story is told that Cloud Man was caught in a great blizzard far out in the Missouri country sometime in the late 1820's. His little hunting party had only a few handfuls of jerked buffalo meat — and their blankets — between themselves and death on the frozen prairies. Under his robes, buried in the snow, Cloud Man reflected on a conversation he had had at Fort Snelling with Major Taliaferro. The Agent had pointed out the precariousness of the old Indian hunting way of life as contrasted with the safety and settled advantages of agriculture.

Then and there, Cloud Man made up his mind that if ever he got back to Minnesota

he would plant corn and wheat, Christianize his people and try to mould them to the white man's ways. No small order for a Sioux! On his return he found the enthusiastic support and encouragement of Major Taliaferro easy to obtain.

Taliaferro appointed Philander Prescott, Indian trader and former clerk to the Fort Snelling sutler, as government farmer for the Lake Calhoun Indians. A small Indian farming community, named Eatonville, in honor of John H. Eaton, Secretary of War under President Andrew Jackson, sprang up. Here the first sod was broken for agricultural purposes in Hennepin County outside the immediate confines of Fort Snelling.

On the first of May, 1831, Taliaferro rode out to Eatonville and was pleased with what he saw. "I went to Lake Calhoun — Eatonville the agricultural establishment formed for the Medawakanton, and other Sioux," he recorded in his journal. "Took with me hoes — axes etc. for the Indians. I found most of them at work — cutting down trees — grubbing out the roots etc. — what was more encouraging — some few of the men were at this unusual kind of labor for them. They laughed when they saw me. I

praised them in every agreeable way that could be conveyed to them in their language."

But Cloud Man's village at Lake Calhoun, on the trail to the Minnesota River, was exposed to war raids of the hostile Chippewas. Later it was moved south of the Minnesota River. Cloud Man was one of the signers of the treaties of 1837, of Traverse des Sioux in 1851 and the Washington treaty of 1858. He refused to take part in the Sioux Uprising of 1862, and the following winter died at the Sioux internment camp at Fort Snelling.

Samuel Pond, the famous frontier missionary who knew Cloud Man well, said of him: "It would have been well for the Dakotas if they had had more chiefs like him, but he was far in advance of his contemporaries and was the only chief who was decidedly in favor of abandoning the chase and cultivating the arts of civilized life. He was a man of superior discernment, and of great prudence and foresight. He did not hesitate to tell the Dakotas that the time had come when nothing but a change in their mode of life could save them from ruin, yet they were very slow to adopt his new notions."

The Way We Lived Then-I

Some time in the late spring of 1851 an observant young man named Eli Pettijohn went out to Mendota to see Henry Sibley and was invited to stay for dinner. Sibley was the region's leading fur trader. He was to be the state of Minnesota's first governor. Affable, friendly, courteous, he shared with most frontiersmen a genius for hospitality.

Mr. Sibley lived in what the west considered a large house, built six years before of native stone. For the time and place, he lived elegantly. He was waited on by Indians. His home was furnished in massive mohogany and young Pettijohn was over-awed by his bountiful table.

After feasting on what he thought was a fine, juicy, tender roast of beef, Pettijohn caught his host's gaze fixed on him questioningly.

"I suppose," Mr. Sibley observed, "you know what this is."

"Yes," Pettijohn replied, "It is the finest roast beef I have ever tasted."

Mr. Sibley shook his head.

"No," he explained, "this is what we call boss of buffalo. It is the hump on the back of a young male buffalo."

The great staple food of the frontier was pemmican. This was dried buffalo or venison (sometimes other animals), pounded fine and frequently flavored with powdered wild cherries, a trick learned from the Indians. The meat was put in a buffalo skin sack and melted fat was poured over the whole mass. It would keep indefinitely. Men did vast labors, traveled Odyssean journeys, on pemmican. It was one of the most nourishing foods ever concocted. For years it was the mainstay in the diet of all frontiersmen, explorers, trappers and hunters. It helped build the American West.

Whatever it was, Pettijohn replied, it was the best meat he had ever tasted.

Sibley went on, indicating another dish and asking if Pettijohn knew what that was. Pettijohn thought it was dried beef, probably the tastiest he had eaten. It turned out, however, to be boned, dried beaver tail — a great delicacy of the frontier, one of the favorite dishes of the Sioux Indians.

But in the west the traveler rarely dined at sumptuous mahogany boards like Henry Sibley's. More often there was hardtack and pea and pork stew, cooked by the river men all night over hot coals in a hole in the ground, covered over with earth. It was a rich, tasty dish and nourishing but nothing epicurean. If one were lucky there was tea, brought north on the river boats. And maple sugar purchased from the Indians.

Men Remembered the Falls.

Speeding across Third Avenue bridge in a high-powered modern automobile it is almost impossible to get a good view of St. Anthony Falls today. And even if you do stop, get out and look, present-day developments in and around the river have obscured the original majesty of the falls. Visitors to the city·sometimes ask, if their disappointment is keen enough to blunt their manners, "But where are the falls?"

Why, then, were the falls so impressive to early travelers? Why were they one, of the great wonders of the early west? Why did the Indians weave legends about them, believing that they were a dwelling place of gods? Many men saw the falls at an early day and many left records of their impressions. The answers to these questions may be found in the writings of early visitors to the Minneapolis area.

Several things about St. Anthony Falls seemed to hit early viewers. One was their vast breadth — more than 600 yards from bank to bank. Then, there was the wild picturesque beauty of the surrounding country. Here the prairies broke abruptly into rough rock and river gorge. Finally, there was loneliness and isolation about the falls and this, it would appear, left a deep impression on most of its pioneer visitors.

William H. Keating, mineralogist and chemist who accompanied the Long expedition up the Minnesota River in 1823, has left one of the best descriptions of the falls.

"We discovered," he wrote, "that nothing could be more picturesque than this cascade. We had been told that it appeared like a mere mill-dam, and we were apprehensive lest a fall of sixteen feet would lose all its beauty when extended upon a breadth of several hundred yards: but we soon observed that this was by no means the case.

"The irregular outline of the fall," Keating continued. "by dividing its breadth, gives a more impressive character . . . this fall is subdivided into small cascades, which adhere to each other, so as to form a sheet of water, unrent, but composed of an alternation of retiring and salient angles, and presenting a great variety of shapes and shades; each of these forms in itself a perfect cascade, but when taken together in one comprehensive view, they assume a beauty of which we could scarcely deem them susceptible. We have

seen many falls, but few which present a wilder and more picturesque aspect than those of St. Anthony."

Three years before Keating, Henry Rowe Schoolcraft, the famed Indian authority from whom Longfellow borrowed many ideas for Hiawatha, came down the river and remarked the impressiveness of the falls.

"Nothing can exceed the beauty of the prairies which skirt both banks of the river above the falls," he wrote. ". . . in the spring and fall, this cataract attains a character of sublimity, from the increased volume and tumult of the water, and the inundation of the accumulated debris, which presents, at this season, so rugged an aspect . . . this accession of water produces a cloud of spray . . ."

E. S. Seymour, who saw the falls in the summer of 1849 and later wrote a book about Minnesota Territory which he called the New England of the West, said that "the rapids commence many rods above the perpendicular fall, the water foaming and boiling with great violence whenever it meets a rock or other obstruction.

"Reaching the verge of the cataract," Seymour continued, "it precipitates itself from a perpendicular height of sixteen and a half feet. Such a large volume of water, falling that distance, would naturally produce emotions of grandeur in the mind of the beholder.

"Here the effect is heightened by the air of desolation and evidence of violence which the scenery presents. Huge masses of rock, gigantic blocks of limestone, heaped one upon another, and strewed about immediately below the Falls, in a circular form, and, still farther below, in confused heaps, attract the attention of the spectator, inspire him with feelings of awe, and lead his mind into a train of solemn reflections. . ."

Long before white men came this way, the Sioux had stood in awe of the Mississippi cataract. One old Indian story tells of a young mother who carried her children to death over the falls. Deserted by her husband, who had run off with another woman, the Sioux girl got in her canoe, taking her children with her, and chanted her death song as the rushing waters carried her to oblivion. The Sioux believed that at night the misty form of the young mother and her children floated in the spray above the falls, that the rush of the waters echoed the last sad notes of her song.

Whatever the legends, whatever the "solemn reflections" of other men, one man saw the falls of the future — and prepared to do something about them. This was the keen-eyed sutler at Fort Snelling, Franklin Steele.

31

Franklin Steele

THE MAN FROM THE POST EXCHANGE.

Modern GIs would call Franklin Steele "the man from the post exchange" but to the frontier army he was the "sutler" at Fort Snelling. He had good connections. He was Henry Sibley's brother-in-law.

According to the practice of those days, the sutler, working on contract with the army, ran a kind of general store for the garrison. Soldiers could buy from him most of the things they needed to make a hard life a little more pleasant — fishing tackle or a package of needles, dried apples or a pound of butter, shoes or sealing wax. Whatever it was, the sutler had it.

Steele was twenty-four years old when he came out to Fort Snelling in 1837. He was a native of Pennsylvania. President Andrew Jackson, stealing a march on Horace Greeley, had advised him to "go west, young man." He had a native astuteness, a shrewd flair for business. It took no time at all to make up his mind on the importance of the water power at St. Anthony Falls.

Steele's claim to the eastern bank of the river at the falls is the subject of a number of stories. Probably none can now be authenticated beyond a shadow of doubt. He may have had advance information on the ratification of Indian treaties that opened land to settlement. One story goes that he raced up river, carrying a sack of potatoes which he "planted" to prove he had the land under cultivation.

32

Another story is that Steele outraced Major Joseph Plympton, commanding officer at Fort Snelling in 1838, to stake a claim at the falls when the Indian treaty news came through from the east. Plympton and Steele received the news at approximately the same time but Plympton decided to wait until the next day. He couldn't have known Franklin Steele too well. Next morning, when he arrived, he found the sutler with a shack up and a corn field "planted." The stories vary but one fact is plain: Steele won the race to the falls.

Franklin Steele flourished. In 1840 he was commissioned postmaster at Fort Snelling, the first in what now is the state of Minnesota. In 1847-48 he built a sawmill, the first privately owned mill at St. Anthony Falls. He opened a store in the new community. In 1851, after the creation of Minnesota Territory, he was appointed a member of the first board of regents of the University of Minnesota. He donated a land tract in St. Anthony for university use. When the panic of 1857 struck he advanced funds from his own pocket for the university. He was the main promoter of the first suspension bridge and at one time he owned Fort Snelling. The government actually paid him "rent" for use of the old frontier post during the Civil War.

A shrewd, enterprising gentleman, this man from the post exchange. Colonel John H. Stevens, his friend and associate, once said of him: "He was the foremost business man in this part of the Northwest."

PIERRE BOTTINEAU

Minneapolis' own Davy Crockett.

Pierre Bottineau

Pierre Bottineau, the half-breed scout who hunted, trapped and guided all over the old northwest in the three decades before the Civil War, was the kind of a man who left indelible memories in the minds of other men. There are still old-timers in the city who remember their fathers' tales about Pierre Bottineau — how he used to skip silver dollars on the Mississippi River.

Bottineau was born at a Red River fur-trading post in 1817, the son of a French fur trader and a Chippewa mother. Most of his early life was spent among the Chip-

pewa Indians. He developed into a fabulous marksman and a skillful hunter. While still a boy he became a guide to explorers and prospectors.

Restless like most frontiersmen, he drifted in and out of the border settlements. In 1845 he came to St. Anthony Falls, then still a hang-out for the mixed-blood children of the fur trade. He bought a claim, adjoining Franklin Steele's on the north.

For about eight or nine years he was in and around St. Anthony. In 1849 he donated the site for St. Anthony of Padua church. In the early 1850's he staked another claim in rural Hennepin county, on the present site of Osseo, which was long known as Bottineau's prairie.

Through the 1850's Pierre Bottineau guided military parties establishing frontier forts. He was scout for Colonel W. H. Noble's wagon road expedition to the Frazer River. In 1860 he went with Governor Alexander Ramsey to the northern Chippewa country. He guided the Fisk Idaho expedition and Sibley's army against the Sioux in 1862.

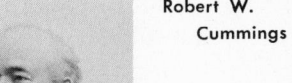

THE SHAPE OF THINGS TO COME.

From the earliest times Americans had been pushing west. By the 1840's the westward movement was washing up in ever higher and higher waves on the shores of the upper Mississippi. In 1847 a government land office was opened at St. Croix Falls, Wisconsin Territory, and the county between the St. Croix and Mississippi rivers was declared ready for settlement.

This precipitated "the boom of 1847" at St. Anthony Falls. That year saw the arrival of many persons whose names were to be written large in the early history of the community. Ard Godfrey, an accomplished millwright whom Franklin Steele had obtained from Maine, came out to the western country to build Steele's new sawmill at the falls.

There were others. William Cheever arrived to stake a claim near what is now the University of Minnesota campus. In the early days the little community that sprang up around him was known as "Cheevertown." He built a tower looking out on a magnificent view of the river and the falls.

It carried a sign: "Pay your dime and climb."

In the early spring of 1847, before the frost was out of the ground, a future governor and Civil War hero, William R. Marshall, packing all his belongings on his back, hiked overland from the St. Croix River to St. Anthony Falls. Later he was to be a colonel of the Seventh Minnesota Infantry in the Sioux Uprising and in the Civil War. He was governor of the state from 1866 to 1870. For many years he was prominent in the business life of the community as banker, merchant, real estate man and newspaper editor.

The same year Luther P. Patch, his wife, two daughters and a son arrived and moved into Franklin Steele's log cabin. Mrs. Patch and the daughters, Marian and Cora, were the first white women who were permanent residents of what now is the city of Minneapolis. Marian was the community's first bride. On October 3, 1848, she was married to Roswell P. Russell, who had been a trader at Fort Snelling and who became the

city's first merchant by opening a small general store the year of his marriage.

The boom of '47 brought in other well-known names — Caleb Dorr, Calvin Tuttle, Sumner W. Farnham, Daniel Stanchfield, Charles W. Stimpson, Robert W. Cummings, Samuel Ferrald, John McDonald and John Rollins.

Most of these people had New England backgrounds. They tried to re-create something that would remind them of home. Very soon, St. Anthony took on the little-white-house look of a New England village. The new mill, open in 1848, poured out a plentiful supply of building material and soon there were stores and shops along the main street. St. Anthony was definitely "in business."

But across the river, on the west side, the government beef herd was still pastured at the Old Government mills. The land was closed to settlement. Smoke still rose from Sioux lodges. Only a few Indians and the Army could call the west side "home."

St. Anthony, 1856

Ard Godfrey

ARD GODFREY --- the man who built the mill

When Franklin Steele's title to river front property became firmly secure in 1847, the Fort Snelling sutler, who had long had a sharp eye on the water power of St. Anthony Falls, sent east for a millwright, Ard Godfrey.

Godfrey had grown up in the Maine sawmills. He had learned his trade from a millwright father. When he arrived at the falls he was a vigorous 34-year-old, well prepared to put a mill into operation in record time.

Steele wasted no time on the project. Even before Godfrey arrived the sutler had **timber cut on Nicollet Island** and handhewn to build a dam and mill frame. More timber was floated down river in the spring of 1848. When completed the new mill had two saws and could cut about 15,000 feet of lumber a day.

When a post office was open in St. Anthony later that year, Godfrey became the first postmaster. He was one of the charter members of the Masonic lodge (Cataract) organized in 1851.

In the 1850's Godfrey staked a claim on the west side of the river, near Minnehaha Falls, and built a sawmill on Minnehaha Creek. He had a wharf on the river front at the creek's outlet, which was then known as Godfrey's Point.

Godfrey's house, built in 1848 of lumber cut at the sawmill and one of the first frame houses on the eastern side of the river, was presented to the city in 1909. It stood originally at Main and Pine (now Second) Streets but was moved later to the square at Central and University Avenues.

Col. John N. Stevens

First Across the River - - - COLONEL JOHN H. STEVENS

In Minnesota's early days many people found it profitable to take a jaunt out to the square stone house at Mendota to have a talk with Henry Sibley, the fur trader. In the spring of 1849 a young veteran of the Mexican War, just arrived from down river, saw Sibley and received a piece of information that was to influence the rest of his life. The young man was John H. Stevens. Sibley told him the sutler at Fort Snelling, Franklin Steele, needed a bookkeeper.

Stevens had been born in Lower Canada in 1820. His parents were natives of Vermont. He came west as a youth and worked in the lead mines at Galena, Ill. When the Mexican War came along he enlisted in the army.

The busy sutler at Fort Snelling, with more plans than you could shake a stick at, was as Henry Sibley reported, on the look-out for a bright young man. Stevens was hired as a bookkeeper and went to work in the sutler's store. Within a matter of weeks he was Steele's confidential agent and intimate friend.

At that time the west bank of the river was still closed to settlement. It lay within the military reservation of Fort Snelling. But as usual Franklin Steele had ideas. The military road from Fort Snelling to Fort Gaines (Ripley) was on the east side of the river above St. Anthony Falls. Troops and supplies, leaving Fort Snelling, had to make a perilous crossing, fording the river above the falls.

Two years earlier Steele had established a ferry near the site of the present Hennepin Avenue bridge. Steele's proposal now was that Stevens make application to live on the west river bank with the understanding that he would maintain the ferry for free Government use. The application was endorsed by Lt. Col. Gustav Loomis, then commanding Fort Snelling, and bore the recommendations of both Franklin Steele and Henry Sibley. After years of saying "no" the War Department in Washington finally approved the first permanent non-military resident of Minneapolis.

"Thus," wrote Colonel Stevens in his memoirs years later, "through the engagement with Mr. Steele, I became an occupant of the land that I had so much admired a few weeks before on the occasion of my first visit to the falls. . . . There, on the bank of the river, just above the rapids, I commenced building my humble house, to which, when finished, I brought my wife as a bride, and in it my first children were born, the eldest being the first-born child in Minneapolis proper."

The following year Stevens cleared forty acres of land and planted wheat, corn and oats. The crops flourished — an important point because many people then believed grains could not be successfully grown so far north. Stevens also established a herd of cows. His farm was the first on the western side of the river north of the Iowa line.

In 1852 the Fort Snelling military reservation was reduced and a short time later Colonel Stevens secured clear title to his land. Hennepin County was organized in his house and the first county election was held there. Colonel Stevens himself was elected first Hennepin County register of deeds. Subsequently, he served several terms in the Minnesota legislature.

CAP TAPPER - he paddled the river and watched the bridge

At Right: Cap Tapper

Early accounts of John Tapper say that he had leathery, hard sinewed arms. He needed them. He was the ferryman and in the early days the "ferry" was a rowboat or a canoe. It took a strong man to pull or paddle across current without going over the falls.

John Tapper was born in East Orange, Dorsetshire, England, in 1820. He was twenty years old when he came to America. He had a brother working at Fort Atkinson, Iowa, and got a job there driving an army six-mule team. In 1842 he went to Fort Crawford at Prairie du Chien, and two years later he came up river to Fort Snelling, still working as an army mule skinner. He went south with the Fort Snelling sur-

geon during the Mexican War but returned to the fort in 1847.

Everybody called him "Captain," perhaps because he was a nautical man of sorts, but there is no record of an official army or navy commission in his name. With old Pierre Bottineau he helped build the Stevens house. When the first suspension bridge was opened in 1855, John Tapper got the job as tollgate keeper.

He stayed on for seven years and then, in 1862, he moved south to try a little farming in Iowa. Like many another man on the frontier, John Tapper had an itching foot. He returned to Minnesota in later life and died at the home of a son, Frank Tapper, at Villard, Minn., March 5, 1909.

The little village of St. Anthony was one of the ports of call for the Red River carts, the first prairie schooners of the old northwest country. Each year through the 1840's and 1850's these big, two-wheeled carts, driven by Red River metis—half-breeds—rumbled and squeaked their way over the prairies carrying rich cargoes of furs and supplies between the northern outposts, Pembina and Fort Garry (Winnipeg) and St. Paul.

Caleb Dorr, one of the pioneers of St. Anthony who was boarding with the Ard Godfreys about 1850, has left us a picture of what the arrival of the Red River drivers meant in the frontier settlement.

"The Red River carts used to come down from Fort Garry loaded with furs," he wrote. "The drivers were half-breeds, sons of the traders and hunters. They always looked more Indian than white. These cart drivers generally wore buckskin clothes tricked out so as to make them gay. As there was not much to amuse us, we were always interested to see the carts and their squawking was endured, as it could not be cured. It could be heard three miles away. They came down the Main road, afterwards called the Anoka road."

When a Red River brigade arrived at St. Anthony there always was music and dancing. Part French, the Red River drivers were born with a love of fiddle music and song. Settlers frequently were challenged to endurance dances. These often went on into the early hours of the morning. Caleb Dorr,

The Way We Lived Then - II

caught in one such challenge, remarked: "I danced until my teeth rattled and I saw stars."

The old Mess House on the east bank of the river, a few yards upstream from the present site of the Third Avenue bridge, was a center of the little social activity the village had. Built for the men who worked on the mills, the Mess House — sometimes called the Soap Grease Exchange (the butter often was rancid) — also served as a restaurant for travelers.

St. Anthony also had a little slab house down near the falls called the "Strangers' House." Newcomers were welcome to stay there until they had homes of their own. Hastily put together, the house had many chinks. These were convenient peepholes

for curious Indians. One early arrival recalled "there were always rows of bright Indians' eyes like beads on a string watching us through these cracks."

Frontier youngsters played with Indian children. The Sioux had a camp at the mouth of Bassett's creek. Many a white boy learned to hunt, fish and trap from the Indians. Years later Dr. Lysander P. Foster recalled: "I spent many happy days hunting, fishing and playing games with them. They were always fair in their play. The games they enjoyed most were 'shinny' and a game played on the ice in winter. A stick with a long handle and heavy smooth curved end was thrown with all the strength possible. . . the one throwing it farthest beat. I suppose what I call 'shinny' was really LaCrosse."

A CITY IS BORN . . . 1852-1856

C. W. Christmas

Soon after Colonel Stevens built his little house above the falls, ambitious settlers began to squat on the military reservation. Some of them obtained permits from the War Department.

Out at Lake Calhoun Charles Mosseau, a French-Canadian voyageur for the American Fur Company, settled down on the southeast shore. The Rev. E. G. Gear, chaplain at the fort, staked a claim farther north on the east shore. A dozen men moved across the river from the east side.

The creation of the Minnesota Territory in 1849 and the growing certainty that settlement could not be stopped in its steady westward march, brought a rush of squatters over the river. Sometimes they were evicted by troops from Fort Snelling. Sometimes their shanties were burned down or their lumber and logs thrown into the river.

At last in August, 1852, President Millard Fillmore signed an act of Congress reducing the Fort Snelling military reservation. The way was open for permanent, legal settlement on the western side of the river.

"Unfortunately," Colonel Stevens wrote later, "the law passed by Congress reducing the Fort Snelling reservation contained no provision for the relief of settlers on the land, thus causing us great anxiety in regard to the future title to our homes. A claim association was instantly organized. Stringent rules were adopted against claim jumpers, and others who might wish to interfere with our claims. The severe measures taken by the association were of such a character that no one would be sure of his life who should attempt to jump a claim."

One instance of vigilantism by the "Equal Right and Impartial Protection Claim Association of Hennepin County, Minnesota Territory" has been recorded. A claim jumper was discovered near Minnehaha Falls. Irate citizens of the Equal Right group visited him with a cat o' nine tails which was vigorously applied to his bare back. That ended claim jumping.

In May, 1855, by a further act of Congress, the settlers obtained clear title to 19,773 acres — most of what is now south Minneapolis — for $24,668.37.

Even before this, however, Colonel Stevens, certain that title would become clear, had had one hundred acres surveyed for a townsite by Charles W. Christmas. He began giving away lots to people who would build. Because he had known New Orleans in his youth and had been impressed by it, Colonel Stevens had Minneapolis laid out as he remembered the new sections of New Orleans in the 1840's. In March, 1856, the territorial legislature incorporated Minneapolis.

40

Minneapolis, 1856

41

100 YEARS LATER — the city as it appears today from the St. Anthony side of the Mississippi River. Just a century ago this was river cliff and rolling prairie with a few scattered houses and Sioux tepees dotting the landscape. Not even the most optimistic pioneer could have envisaged it as it is today.

How Minneapolis Got Its Name.

Charles Hoag

The little community clustered around the falls on the west bank of the river was in search of a name. By 1852, the first Hennepin county board of commissioners thought they had it — Albion, because the settlers mostly were of English descent.

But there were many other ideas — Lowell, Hennepin, All Saints, Brooklyn, Addiesville. None seemed quite right. They just didn't fit.

Then, on the morning of November 5, 1852, a school teacher from New England, Charles Hoag, who had bought the old Bassett claim for $100, appeared at the office of the St. Anthony Express just as it was going to press. He had a letter for the editor, George D. Bowman. Bowman was so impressed that he held the paper, hurriedly set new type and inserted the Hoag letter.

"The name I propose," Hoag had written,

"Minnehapolis (is) derived from Minnehaha (laughing water) with the Greek affix, polis (a city), meaning 'Laughing Water City' or 'City of the Falls' — you perceive I spell it with an 'h' which is silent in the pronunciation."

The name caught on immediately. A week later, Bowman printed an editorial in the Express plumping for "Minnehapolis" and because of this he sometimes has been given credit, erroneously, for naming the city.

A short time later there was a meeting of settlers at Colonel Stevens' house. The Colonel, years afterward, wrote that ". . . from the appearance of Mr. Hoag's article . . . the Anglo-Saxon 'Albion' was doomed . . . It was finally settled at an accidental meeting of most all the citizens at my house in December, 1852. It was decided to withdraw the silent 'h' and call the place 'Minneapolis'."

Man of the Century...

The history of a community such as Minneapolis, or of a company such as Cargill, Inc., <u>can</u> be interestingly told in terms of buildings, of physical development—and that is the way it is often told.

Neither Minneapolis nor Cargill can, however, fully tell the 100-year story in terms of buildings, property, or other purely physical objects. The dramatic account of the building of the Northwest, and Minneapolis the center of that area, is the story of a man, The Farmer.

The greatness of Minneapolis is inseparably tied to the milling industry. Here is the milling center of the world and it is the farmer who has been, and continues to be, the leading figure in that center.

For more than 90 years, almost the entire 100 years of Minneapolis' existence, Cargill has been serving the farmer and the milling industry. The growth of the farmer and of the milling industry has made possible our growth. This is as it should be since we have ever been glad to be in the No. 2 position on the farmer-processor team.

As farming has become more complex and the farmer's needs more complex, too, Cargill has become more diversified. The farmer now draws upon us in many ways—from service at country elevators to using our feeds and hybrid corn, to using the many products resulting from our creative processing.

Cargill has grown through service to the farmer and—it may be said—this is likewise the story of Minneapolis in this its Centennial year.

90 Years of Creative Processing of Farm Products CARGILL

The Beginnings
of Government.

Dorilus Morrison

Like so many other things in Minneapolis, the beginnings of government go back to old Fort Snelling. In the early days the administration and enforcement of law centered in the Fort's commanding officer and the Indian agent.

By 1849, Minnesota territory had been created and three years later the territorial legislature set up Hennepin county. In 1855 the "City of St. Anthony" on the east side of the river was incorporated and Henry T. Welles was elected mayor.

On March 1, 1956, Governor Willis A. Gorman approved an act incorporating the "Town of Minneapolis." This irked dwellers on the river's western bank. Why should they be a "town" while their neighbors across the river were a "city"?

Ten years later the state legislature incorporated Minneapolis as a city but there was so much disagreement over boundaries and the inclusion or exclusion of St. Anthony that the act failed to become effective. The following year another act of incorporation was passed and on February 19, 1867, Dorilus Morrison, a Maine stater who had come to St. Anthony in 1854, was elected mayor.

Fifty-two years old at the time, Morrison already was prominent in the community. He had learned the lumber outfitting business in Maine. When he came to St. Anthony he pursued it further. He got into the sawmill business, opened a lumber yard and spread his activities to all phases of lumbering. Before his election as mayor, he had been a member of the state legislature. He was elected mayor again in 1869.

NOW FOR THE NEXT 100 YEARS

New Blackdog Power Plant, generates 270,000 KW, enough electricity to light 540,000 homes.

NSP shares Minneapolis' confidence in an even greater future . . . and is building for it!

ONE HUNDRED YEARS ago . . . a tiny settlement. Today an important cosmopolitan city . . . 17th largest in the nation . . . looking forward to another century of progress . . . confident of an even more prosperous future.

Northern States Power Company shares that confidence and is proving it with a never-ending building program. In the last 10 years NSP has invested $327 million in new construction and has more than doubled the electric supply for this area.

In the next three years NSP will invest $117,000,000 ($40,000,000 in 1956 alone) in new facilities of all kinds to assure you all the electricity you want—and more!

Planning, working, building with Minneapolis, NSP keeps ahead of your ever-increasing need for electric service . . . now and for the *next* 100 years.

Building to match Minneapolis' progress

NORTHERN STATES
NSP
POWER COMPANY

For The "Shattered Thunderbolt"----

Two Companies.

When Abraham Lincoln called for 75,-000 volunteers to put down rebellion in the spring of 1861 Minnesota was the first state to respond — and the First Minnesota became one of the most famous regiments of the Civil War. In the opinion of many military experts it was one of the greatest combat units in the history of the American armed services.

Minneapolis and St. Anthony Falls furnished two companies to what later became known as "the Shattered Thunderbolt" (it suffered 82 per cent casualties at the battle of Gettysburg, probably the highest casualty percentage figure in the Union armies for the entire war). In Minneapolis, Captain Henry R. Putman raised Company D for the First Minnesota, and across the river in St. Anthony, Captain George N. Morgan organized Company E.

The Falls communities were full of young men—the hard handed, hard bellied youngsters who were building the west — lumberjacks, sawmill workers, rivermen, teamsters, homestead seekers — just the kind of men the Army's drill sergeants needed. Out of a total population of 7,000 on both sides of the river, Minneapolis and St. Anthony sent almost 1,400 men to the Union armies.

Enlistments boomed at the time of the Sioux Uprising in the summer of 1862. Sioux war parties approached to within a few miles of the city on the west. Men from Minneapolis and St. Anthony flocked to the colors of the Sixth, Seventh, Tenth and Eleventh infantry regiments which were raised in rapid order.

Out on the plains of the Missouri, north along the Canadian border, east by the Chickahominy and James, south in the canebrakes of Arkansas Minneapolis men fought and died in the next four years. Some of them launched careers that were to lead to state and national eminence.

When it was all over, the national hero, General Ulysses S. Grant, on triumphal tour, came out to the developing city on the upper Mississippi. It was a time of optimism and burgeoning hope. Horace Greeley, the famous editor of the New York Tribune, summed things up when he spoke at the Minnesota State Fair (held in 1865 in Minneapolis) : ". . . Minneapolis has advantages enough in her enormous yet most facile water power, which may be made to give employment to a population of 100,000 souls . . ."

When The Sawmills Roared.

The great pine forests of northern Minnesota, plus the water power of St. Anthony Falls, gave the city its first big industrial boom. At the turn of the century, Minneapolis was the greatest lumber producing center in the United States. In 1900 Minneapolis mills sawed more than $12,250,000 worth of lumber.

Demands for lumber through the last half of the Nineteenth Century came in from all over the nation. As American expansion peopled the treeless plains of the west and southwest Minneapolis mills sawed day and night to keep up with the orders.

Many famous Minneapolis names were associated with the lumber business — Franklin Steele, Ard Godfrey, Caleb Dorr, Richard Chute, the Bassetts, the Days, the Lovejoys, Sumner W. Farnham, the Washburns, the Morrisons, T. B. Walker, B. F.

Nelson, E. W. Backus, Thomas H. Shevlin, E. L. Carpenter, Hovey C. Clark, the Wintons, Charles A. Bovey, John De Laittre, and there were many more.

Logs from northern Minnesota could be floated directly to the sawmills that lined the river around St. Anthony Falls. At the height of the lumber era Minneapolis was sawing more than half a billion feet of lumber each year.

Beginning in 1901, the annual "drives" tapered off. By 1915 the total output of Minneapolis mills was only slightly more than a tenth of what it had been when the century opened. Today, although the old sawmills are gone, lumber and the hundreds of articles derived from forest products by the magic of modern technology, are still major factors in the economic life of the community.

Joel B. Bassett

Richard Chute

Thomas H. Shevlin

Edward W. Backus

John De Laittre

Charles A. Bovey

50

ideas build great cities

B. F. NELSON

Minneapolis was a frontier town, back in 1856. A small mill started by the water power of St. Anthony Falls, formed the first industry of this area. Minneapolis men realized the significance of this power, and with their own resource, muscle, and IDEAS, built a city.

B. F. Nelson was a man with an IDEA. In 1865, armed with only $1, but with plenty of ambition, he came to Minneapolis where at first he operated a lumber mill, and afterwards created an industry out of the waste products of the fast growing lumber business. Nelson's IDEA led to the processing of rags into a pulp, saturation with asphalt and coating with granules to produce a high quality roofing material which today is used with confidence and trust.

We at B. F. Nelson look forward with optimism to another 100 years of progress.

Congratulations, Minneapolis, and Thanks to the IDEAS that built a city.

GODFREY HOUSE

Aptly enough, a B. F. Nelson roof preserves the Godfrey House today, oldest dwelling in Minneapolis, first built in 1848, and now protected by a Nelson's Master Roof.

Is it any wonder that Minneapolis is proud of its men of IDEAS?

Nelson's
MASTER ROOFS

THE B. F. NELSON MFG. CO.
MINNEAPOLIS, MINNESOTA

A Quarter Century Ago...
a Sawmill on the Mississippi

Exciting and action-packed is the adventure story of the Scherer brothers, Clarence and Munn, who started their lumber business by harvesting dead-heads from the Mississippi River with an original investment of $240 in 1929. Four years later they bought out a little saw rig and started their milling operations on the east bank of the river.

Today - Millions of Feet of Top Quality Lumber

In 1956 we find that the Scherer Brothers have a 13-acre property on the same site with a storage capacity for millions of feet of lumber in several buildings. Operating one of the largest retail lumber yards in the city, a fleet of ten Scherer Bros. trucks keep the stock rolling steadily to supply the needs of builders of fine homes and commercial buildings in all parts of Minneapolis. This Horatio Alger story is a tribute to the American system of free enterprise and is living proof that there is still opportunity here for young men to achieve success.

TOMORROW

Clarence and Munn Scherer have further plans for expansion of their business in the future and look forward to another quarter century of growth with Minneapolis.

1956

SCHERER BROTHERS LUMBER COMPANY 9TH AVENUE AND THE MISSISSIPPI RIVER

Calvin Tuttle

"Whatever Else Requires Grinding—"

It was an inconspicuous advertisement that appeared in the St. Anthony Express for May 31, 1851, but had men been able to read the future they would have discerned the hand of destiny upon it.

It was headed simply "Grinding" and it read, in part, "The undersigned is now in readiness for grinding Corn, Rye, Oats, Peas, Buckwheat, and whatever else requires grinding, including Salt, at the gristmill on the west side of the Mississippi River at St. Anthony, for lawful rates of toll . . ." It was signed Calvin A. Tuttle.

Tuttle was one of the pioneers of the boom of 1847. At one time he owned most of the present site of the University of Minnesota. In 1849, the old government mill on the west side of the river had been sold to Robert Smith of Illinois who, in turn, rented it to Tuttle.

Whatever Tuttle expected of his operation, there were plenty of frontier wiseacres to tell him he would never get rich grinding wheat in Minnesota. In the early years many people believed that wheat couldn't be grown here in crops big enough to make it profitable. Minnesota was too far north, they said.

Wheat had been grown and flour ground at St. Anthony Falls as early as the 1820's. The red-haired commander of Fort Snelling, Colonel Josiah Snelling, had had the idea first. But Snelling's flour, coarse and poorly ground, had produced a black, bitter tasting bread. It quickly turned mouldy. The soldiers had refused to eat it. A tradition lingered down the years that you couldn't get good flour in Minnesota. There were, however, men who were determined to try.

A year and a half after Tuttle's advertisement appeared the St. Anthony Express carried a brief news note about another "grist mill." This had been built, the Express explained, "by Mr. Rogers, adjoining the Saw Mills, next to Main St. . . . This will be a great advantage to our village and the adjoining country, as there has been a large quantity of grain raised this season . . . Let it be understood that we can make good flour, and production will be so stimulated, that we shall have no need to import any more flour . . ."

This was the real beginning of flour milling at Minneapolis. It has been argued by historians and economists that this one event, more than any other, influenced the whole future development of Minnesota and large sections of the Upper Midwest. There was almost nothing that flour milling did not touch — argiculture, of course; lumbering (to feed the men in the camps); banking, railroads, real estate, manufacturing—in short, practically everything touching the economic life and well-being of the community.

Within forty years after Calvin Tuttle's advertisement Minneapolis was the flour milling capital of the world.

Flour—
Made in Minneapolis

W. D. Washburn

J. S. Pillsbury

John Martin

C. C. Washburn

In the early days Minneapolis millers often labeled their flour barrels "Made in St. Louis." In the East there was no great market for Minneapolis flour and the idea still persisted that Minnesota was too far north to grow really good flour-producing wheat. Hard northern spring wheat was a largely unknown, or even suspect, quantity.

But by the time of the Civil War, the hand of history already was showing in the little communities around St. Anthony Falls. Many of the first lumber men, the sawmill operators and owners, were turning, or would turn in the next few years, to flour milling. Among these were Leonard Day, John S. Pillsbury, Curtis H. Pettit, William P. Ankeny, John Martin, Joel B. Bassett, Dorilus Morrison, William D. and Cadwallader C. Washburn.

Flour was still produced in the age-old,

traditional way, millstone upon millstone. Steel rollers were unknown. The middlings purifier, soon to revolutionize milling, had not been invented. But even with the early methods, flour production at Minneapolis was mounting. Out in the state more land was being plowed and more wheat was pouring into the city. In 1860, the year before the Civil War, four Minneapolis mills produced 30,000 barrels of flour. At the end of the war, seven Minneapolis mills were producing almost 100,000 barrels a year.

By this time the men who were to work "the milling revolution," which was to make Minneapolis the milling capital of the world, were already on the scene. Cadwallader Colden Washburn, a New Englander who had settled at Mineral Point, Wis., had become interested in the falls in 1856. His brother, William D. Washburn,

had arrived a year later. The Washburns had incorporated the Minneapolis Mill Company to control the water power on the west side of the river.

Lawyer, teacher, store clerk, surveyor, "Cad" Washburn was by any standards a remarkable man. He had been elected to congress from Wisconsin in 1855. When the Civil War came along he joined the Second Wisconsin cavalry, became colonel and emerged from the war with the rank of major-general. In 1872 he was elected governor of Wisconsin.

Although not a working miller himself, Governor Washburn was a man of dreams and imagination, wedded to a hard, practical business sense. In 1866 he built the largest mill west of Buffalo, six stories high, of stone, at a cost of $100,000 in Minneapolis. Its capacity was 840 barrels of flour a day — a fabulous figure for those

Speaking of BABY Pictures...

Here's one from the General Mills family album — an engraving of the Washburn Crosby Company's Minneapolis mill in the 1880's. It may not be an artistic triumph, but it's a reminder that General Mills grew up in the city of Minneapolis.

In 1866, Cadwallader C. Washburn, linking his future to the Northwest, built his first mill on the banks of the Mississippi at St. Anthony Falls. Most people called it "Washburn's Folly." They were sure that a six-story mill, costing a fabulous $100,000, could not succeed. Twelve pairs of millstones would flood and overflow the existing markets for flour.

But Cadwallader Washburn knew that, in a young nation, new markets lay just over the horizon. Men of imagination and energy could find them.

Both General Mills and its predecessor Washburn Crosby Company have been crossing those new horizons through the years. While the frontier village in which it was born grew into a city of 530,000 people, General Mills became a nation-wide company serving daily more than 50 million people across America, providing jobs for 13,000 men and women.

Throughout this growth has run the sustaining and unifying belief that prosperity is intimately related to service: the successful company is the one that deserves well by serving well.

General Mills

MINNEAPOLIS, MINNESOTA

General Mills is best known as the world's largest miller, maker of Gold Medal Flour and home of Betty Crocker . . . First Lady of Food. But the company today also produces and provides a myriad of essential products and services, ranging from organic chemicals to electronic machines. For the dramatic story of its birth and growth, read

BUSINESS WITHOUT BOUNDARY *By James Gray*
THE STORY OF GENERAL MILLS

Copies are available from your local bookseller or directly from the University of Minnesota Press, Minneapolis 14, Minnesota.

Cross of Centuries

An old legend tells us that three X's have been the symbol of bread for centuries. Supposedly the symbol "XXX" originally referred to the Crucifixion with each "X" representing one of the crosses on Calvary.

In time medieval millers adopted the mark "XXX" to refer to the best grade of flour for bread, although its use died out long before Pillsbury Flour Mills first came into being.

However, we are told that when Charles A. Pillsbury heard the story he said:

"If three X's mean the best, then we'll add another just to show that Pillsbury's Best is really the best."

That, according to legend, is why the Pillsbury trade mark shows "XXXX." This famous Pillsbury's Best trade mark, together with the dotted circle, was officially registered in 1872 in Washington, D.C.

Pillsbury Mills, Inc.

FLOUR...
made in Minneapolis

James S. Bell

George H. Christian

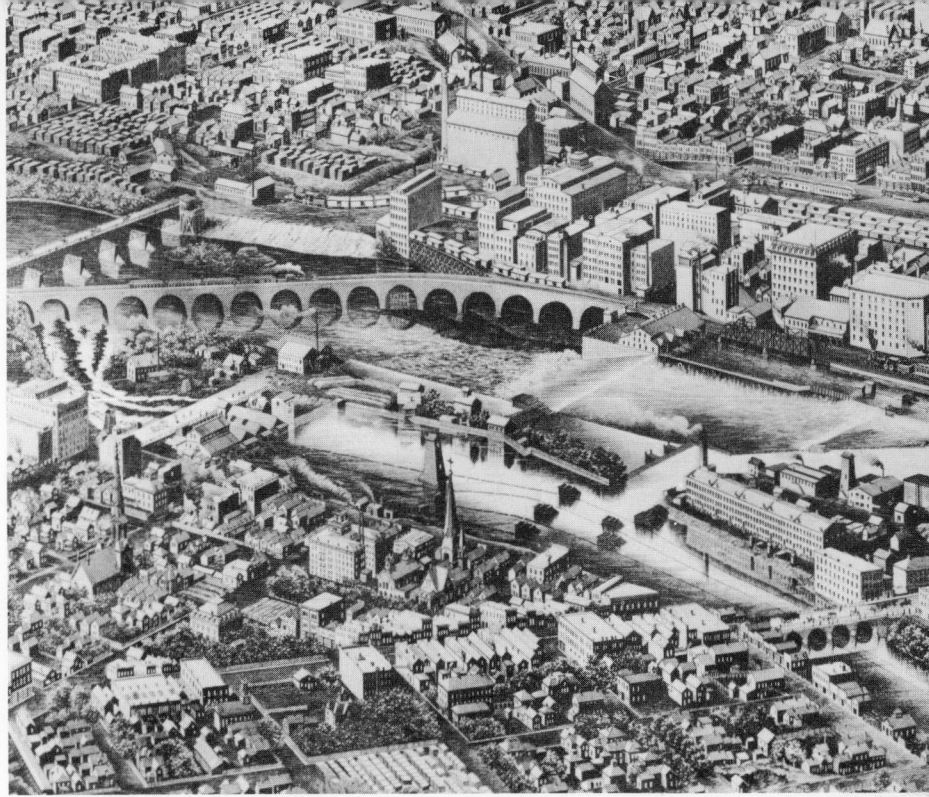

times. Undiscerning men spoke of it as "Washburn's folly."

In 1869, Governor Washburn took on a partner, George Henry Christian, a native Alabaman, who had come north, learned business methods in New York and then moved out to Chicago and Minneapolis as a flour broker. As manager of the Washburn Mill, Christian gave a hearing to Edmund LaCroix, a French inventor, who had come to Minnesota from Canada in 1860. At this time, the mills were still using the old mill-stone methods which, wastefully, produced three products: flour, bran (the outer covering of the wheat berry) and middlings, the coarser particles of flour to which bran stuck.

As a matter of economy, millers had to get more flour from the hard northern wheat. It was the middlings purifier that made this possible. Strictly speaking, La-Croix was not the inventor of the middlings purifier. He had obtained many of his ideas from others in France. But the work he did with Christian at the Washburn Mill paved the way to far reaching developments in the milling industry.

The 1870's came on. Minneapolis began hearing reports that millers in Budapest, Hungary, had discarded millstones and were using steel rollers. Always eager for more knowledge, Governor Washburn went to Budapest in 1877. About the same time,

Charles A. Pillsbury, who with his uncle, John S. Pillsbury and his father, George A. Pillsbury, had formed the Charles A. Pillsbury & Company firm in 1872, also was a European visitor. The idea of the so-called "Hungarian process" (actually Swiss in origin) was getting back to Minneapolis.

Charles Pillsbury went to Hungary and spent two years studying methods of Hungarian millers. The old buhr stones were soon discarded in Minneapolis in both Pillsbury and Washburn mills. In 1881, the huge six-story limestone structure of Pillsbury's A mill rose on the east side of the river. Its capacity was 5,000 barrels of flour a day — a kind of industrial wonder

of its time. By the turn of the century, Minneapolis millers were producing 15,000,000 barrels of flour a year and the product that had once been the poor relation of the milling world was now known as the world's best.

With increasing production, the development of markets for Minneapolis flour became of superlative importance. Governor Washburn sent William Hood Dunwoody to Great Britain to pave the way for British sales. Pillsbury became well known in Europe and finally acquired the reputation as the world's greatest miller. James S. Bell, a Philadelphian who had wide experience

57

MINNEAPOLIS

...HOME OF THE

MILLING INDUSTRY

The development of Minneapolis as a great milling center followed the advent of the roller mill in the early '70's.

Within a few years the Mississippi's banks along the Falls of St. Anthony were crowded with mills even beyond the capacity of the water power. This was, in very truth, the beginning of the golden age in milling.

Seventy-four years ago the first sack of Occident Flour was milled at Valley City, Dakota Territory. From that humble beginning Russell-Miller is, today, one of America's largest milling concerns, with mills in six states and a record of quality products since 1882.

William H. Dunwoody   **Charles A. Pillsbury**

in merchandising flour, joined Washburn, Crosby and Company in 1888.

Down the years the progressive enterprise of the pioneer millers has continued to be a characteristic of the industry. Breakfast foods, cake mixes, biscuit mixes, pancake mixes, and vitamin products now are all part of the milling industry. Laboratory research at the mills constantly is producing new and improved products.

At General Mills what started out to be simply the repair and building of milling machinery has blossomed out into a full-fledged industry of its own — the mechanical division. During World War II, this division was under government contract, producing war materials. Since the war it has moved on into the production of atomic handling equipment and electronics. General Mills laboratories produce the high-altitude, plastic balloons for the famous operation "Sky Hook."

From Calvin Tuttle's modest advertisement in the St. Anthony Express to the latest cake mix is just 105 years. When the modern housewife leaves her super-market with a package of Minneapolis flour in her shopping bag it can truthfully be said that she carries a century of modern industrial history in her hands.

1902...The first plant of the Daniels Linseed Company—forerunner of ADM—was built at Minneapolis in 1902 by John W. Daniels, who was joined the following year by George A. Archer. Both men came from families long associated with flaxseed.

1956...ADM Minneapolis Installation... One of the 111 modern plants and elevators located in 21 states and Canada. ADM manufactures 850 standard products used by every segment of American industry.

Creating New Markets For America's Harvests

From a luxuriant, untamed prairie to a fertile checkerboard of the nation's most productive farms . . . this is the progress achieved during the past 100 years by Midwest people in both agriculture and industry.

As one of the largest processors of agricultural crops, Archer-Daniels-Midland has played an important part in this spectacular development. Each year ADM handles millions of bushels of flaxseed, soybeans, wheat . . . and quantities of other grains. By collecting these crops in country elevators, storing them in great terminals, and routing them to processing plants throughout the world, ADM provides an important service to farmers and industry.

Moreover, ADM's creative research is constantly expanding the horizons of both agriculture and industry. In ADM laboratories, scientists are engaged in a never-ending search for new products from farm crops . . . products that create new markets and greater demand for America's harvests. Products that make life more pleasant for everybody, every day of the year.

Archer-Daniels-Midland company

Archer QUALITY

700 Investors Building, Minneapolis 2, Minnesota

ADM PRODUCTS: LINSEED OIL, SOYBEAN OIL, MARINE OIL, PAINT VEHICLES, RESINS, PLASTICIZERS, FATTY ACIDS, FATTY ALCOHOLS, HYDROGENATED GLYCERIDES, SPERM OIL, FOUNDRY BINDERS, WHEAT FLOUR, INDUSTRIAL CEREALS, VEGETABLE PROTEINS, DEHYDRATED ALFALFA, LIVESTOCK AND POULTRY FEEDS

The Great Mill Disaster

May 2, 1878, was a beautiful, warm spring day — the kind of day on which it is difficult to think of tragedy and disaster — but that evening thousands of Minneapolitans thought the city had been hit by an earthquake. There was a roaring on the wind and families rushed from their homes, seeking safety in the streets. Towards the milling district a pillar of smoke and flame rose skyward. The Washburn A mill had exploded, killing eighteen men.

The force of the blast shattered windows miles away on Summit Avenue in St. Paul. Two nearby mills, the Humboldt and the Diamond, were wrecked along with Washburn A. Three others, the Galaxy, Zenith and Pettit caught fire. So did a nearby shop and lumber yard. It was the worst disaster in Minneapolis' milling history. Glare from the fires lit the sky all night and could be seen for miles away.

Following the explosion University of Minnesota scientists went to work on the problems of flour dust. It was shown that flour dust under certain conditions, and exposed to flame, can be a highly dangerous explosive. Up to that time most mills had been comparatively small and large concentrations of flour dust had not been a problem.

Like many another setback, the Washburn A mill explosion led to new techniques and new machinery. Millers put an end to discharging flour dust into rooms. Dust collectors were invented. Within a few years the mills were entirely free of dust and a repetition of the great disaster became impossible.

...hub of an international milling system

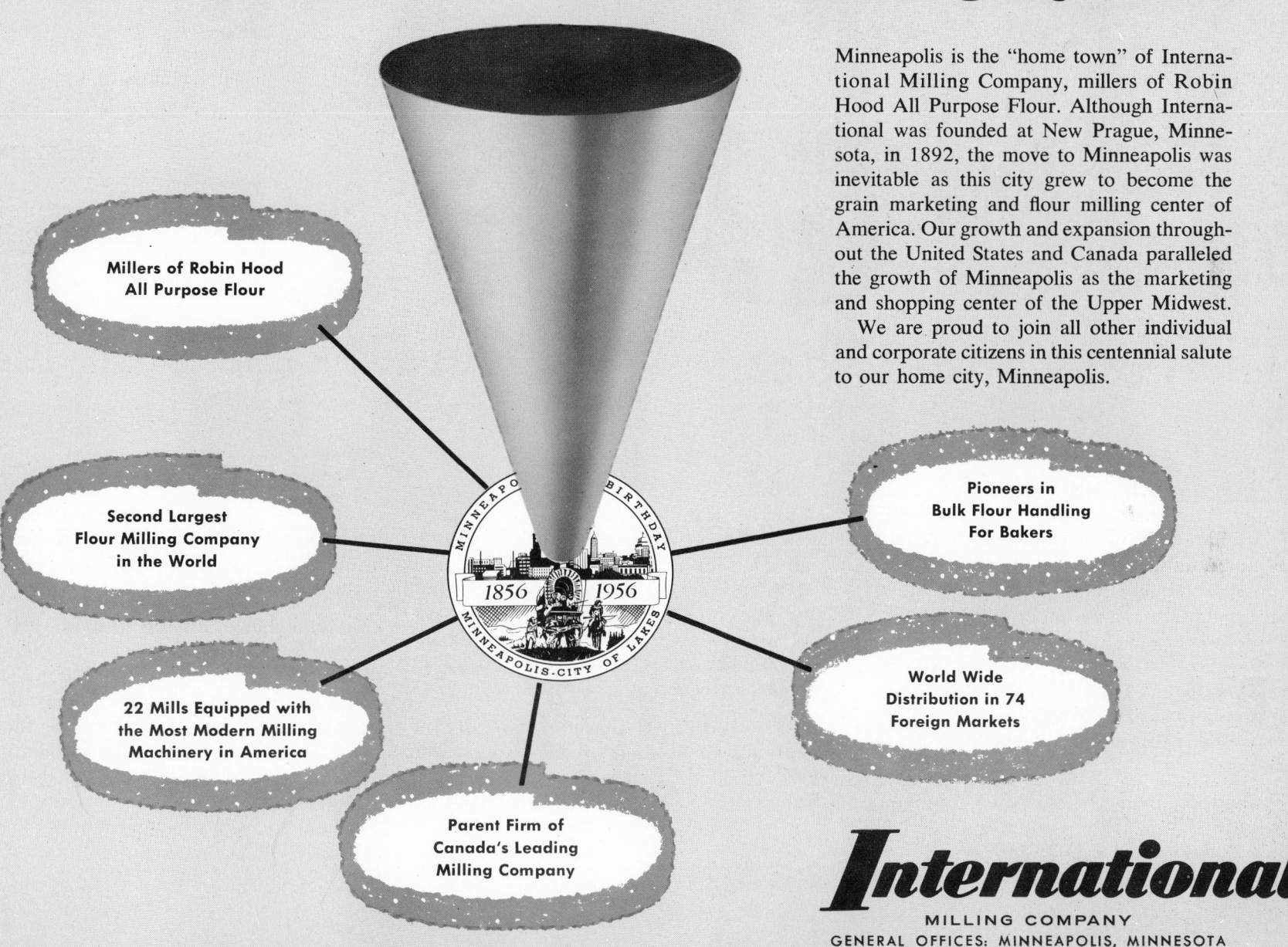

Millers of Robin Hood
All Purpose Flour

Second Largest
Flour Milling Company
in the World

22 Mills Equipped with
the Most Modern Milling
Machinery in America

Parent Firm of
Canada's Leading
Milling Company

Pioneers in
Bulk Flour Handling
For Bakers

World Wide
Distribution in 74
Foreign Markets

MINNEAPOLIS BIRTHDAY
1856 1956
MINNEAPOLIS · CITY OF LAKES

Minneapolis is the "home town" of International Milling Company, millers of Robin Hood All Purpose Flour. Although International was founded at New Prague, Minnesota, in 1892, the move to Minneapolis was inevitable as this city grew to become the grain marketing and flour milling center of America. Our growth and expansion throughout the United States and Canada paralleled the growth of Minneapolis as the marketing and shopping center of the Upper Midwest.

We are proud to join all other individual and corporate citizens in this centennial salute to our home city, Minneapolis.

International
MILLING COMPANY
GENERAL OFFICES: MINNEAPOLIS, MINNESOTA

1863

FLOUR MILLS
Minneapolis

1956

The Day the Bells Rang

October 4, 1869, was a day like all other days in Minneapolis — until the bells rang. Then everybody on both sides of the river rushed down to the water front. Faces turned white at the dread news — "The falls are going out." Off the lower end of Nicollet Island a giant whirlpool, widening ominously, seemed about to carry everything with it to watery destruction.

What had happened was this: More and more industry was trying to use the water power at St. Anthony Falls. Sawmills and flour mills lined both banks. The St. Anthony Falls Water Power Company controlled the east side of the river; the Minneapolis Mill Company controlled the west side. But the islands in the river gave some men ideas about new sources of water power.

William W. Eastman, who had purchased Nicollet Island in 1865, conceived a plan for tunneling from Hennepin to Nicollet islands, allowing some of the swiftly flowing water from the river to pass through the tunnel and thus get power not controlled by the companies on either bank. The tunnel looked like a great idea — but under the limestone edge of the falls there is a bed of soft sandstone. When it became wet, in the

William W. Eastman

tunneling process, it turned to sand and part of the falls gave way.

Every able-bodied man in the two communities rushed to the job of saving the falls. Farmers' loads of hay and wood, waiting sale on Bridge Square, were commandeered and thrown into the river. Rafts were hastily constructed, loaded with stone, and floated out towards the whirlpool only to vanish in the swirling watery pit that seemed bottomless. Two mills and part of a third were carried away.

Hundreds of men joined hurriedly in building coffer dams. Appeals were sent to the federal government in Washington. Congress passed an appropriation bill and government engineers were rushed to Minneapolis. The Eastman tunnel was filled up and a great concrete dike was built across the river, extending fifty feet into the banks on both sides. A heavy crib work, ballasted with stone, was built to protect the crest of the falls. And so Minneapolis' first and most important natural resource was saved.

The Continuing Story of City Government

Minneapolis and St. Anthony were merged in 1872 but the pattern of the city's present government already had been set in the 1867 charter which the legislature gave to Minneapolis.

This provided for elective officers of mayor, treasurer, comptroller, two justices of the peace and twelve aldermen, three from each ward. The mayor had little real power except to appoint the chief of police. He had a veto power but did not sit on the council.

In 1887 the council was increased to thirty-nine members and the power to ap-

point even the police chief was temporarily taken away from the mayor. By 1889 the council was back to twenty-six members and in 1953 it was cut further to thirteen.

In 1891 a strong mayor charter almost became law. It was passed by the legislature at the request of a Democratic Hennepin County delegation, but was vetoed in the last minutes by a Republican governor.

Six attempts to adopt a home rule charter for Minneapolis failed between 1898 and 1920 when a charter embodying essentially the structure the legislature had created was finally adopted. Because of the

severe vote requirements to pass a charter set forth in the constitution, Minneapolitans had begun to despair of ever getting one adopted. When it finally carried in 1920 the vote was 91,000 for and 29,000 against. Women had just obtained the right to vote and were credited with a large part of the victory.

Various groups spearheaded these different charter improvement attempts, including the Charter Union, the Joint Improvement Association, Citizens' Campaign Committee, and the New Charter League. Some of the proposals included strengthening the mayor's office, some maintained the status quo, and one offered the commission form of government. Opposition to change came from public officials, organized labor and some special interest groups.

Dissatisfied with the hodge-podge which had been passed as the city's charter, these and similar groups immediately began agitating for amendments or a new charter. Six amendments were submitted in 1921. Two passed. Shortly thereafter it was decided to try again for a new charter and the Citizens' Representative Charter Commission was organized. After several years of meetings and public discussion, a new city charter setting up a council-manager type of government was presented to the voters. It was soundly defeated in 1926 by 59,360 votes to 27,855.

In the meantime, a central purchasing office for the city was authorized by legislative action in 1911, a civil service system in 1913, and a Board of Estimate and Taxation, a Planning Commission, and a Board of Public Welfare in 1919.

Except for the abolition of ward taxes and street commissioners in 1928 and the establishment of the Housing and Redevelopment Authority in 1947, no changes of consequence have been made in Minneapolis' government since 1919. Compulsory redistricting of wards was passed as a charter amendment in 1946, and in 1948 a complete revision of the city charter, providing for a modified council-manager form of government, was submitted to the voters by the Charter Commission. It was defeated 54,588 to 39,528.

As the city's first century closed, its government was well established in the basic "strong council" pattern adopted ninety years ago, except for the dispersion of some of the strength in a number of semi-independent boards and commissions. In recent years the Minneapolis League of Women Voters and the Citizens' League of Minneapolis and Hennepin County had been active in behalf of charter improvements.

The elongated lithographic print reproduced here is a collector's item. One copy is owned by the Public Library, and there are but two or three others owned by private individuals. Here is a documentary record of each establishment and each business on Washington Avenue in 1882, accurately presented by artist H. A.

WEST CENTRAL PART OF WASHINGTON AVENUE, MINNEAPOLIS, MINN.

Entered according to Act of Congress, in the year 1882, by H. A. Strong, in the Office of the Librarian of Congress, at Washington, D.C.

HENNEPIN AVENUE FIRST AVENUE, NORTH

Tobin, Dry Goods. Simpson & Henderson, Notions, Shirt Makers and Gents' Furnishers. Chicago, St. Paul and Minneapolis Railway Office. Chicago Grand Trunk Daily Freight Office. Bank of Minneapolis, Established 1867. T. W. Wilson, President. American Express Company, Brennen, Starr & Everett, Crockery and Silverware. Security Bank, H. G. Harrison, Vice-Pres. J. W. Tousley & Son, Real Estate Agents. Boston One Price Clothing Store, Academy of Music, King's Jewelry Store. Oscar, the Tailor. J. T. Barnum, Trunk Factory. OSWALD'S BLOCK, Nos. 17 and 19. J. C. Oswald & Co., Wholesale Liquor. W. W. Harrison, Wholesale Grocer, Nos. 17 and 19. Chicago Hotel, J. Leppla, Prop'r. Dick's Restaurant. P. T. Durgin, Commission Merchant. Henry Krueger, Gun Store.

Marshall, Dry Goods. Wolff & Co., Dry Goods. E. G. Barnaby, Druggists. Webster & Churchill, Stone & Hurlburt, Insurance Agents. Chicago, Milwaukee and St. Paul Railway Office. H. C. Webb, Millinery. Dayon & Parker, Real Estate and Loans. Origh & Loan, Real Estate Agents. Hamlin & Brown, Real Estate Agents. Cor. Hennepin and 3d Sts., under Security Bank. Hatter and Men's Furnisher. Nicollet House, John T. West, Prop. Minneapolis Street Railway Office. Sykes & Andrews, Meat Market. Bidwell & Co., Plumbers and Gas Engines.

NICOLLET AVENUE LANE FIRST AVENUE, SOUTH

Corsey & Co., Real Estate & Insurance. First National Bank, J. K. Sidle, Prest. H. G. Sidle, Cashier. J. S. Henton, Boots & Shoes. Y. C. Hutt, Banker & Broker. U. T. K. Clothing Store, No. 210. Ingram, Olsen & Co., Dry Goods and Gents Furnishings. Gale & Co., Real Estate, Loan and Insurance. Barber & Cone, Real Estate. Cushman & Plummer, Book Store. Bay & Co., Grocers. Learned Brothers, Hardware. Beshner Brothers, Gun Store. Nelson Williams, Real Estate and Loans. S. K. Thompson & Co., Real Estate and Insurance. Lawrence & Co., Real Estate. W. Neill, Grocer. P. C. Richardson, Real Estate. W. D. Washburn, Lumber and Flour, Office. J. B. Martin, Drugs and Surgical Instruments. H. G. Harrison & Co., Wholesale Grocers. A. L. Billing & Co., Commission Merchants. Brown's Theatre Costumes.

Eichelzer & Co., Hats, Caps & Furs. Wyman, Mullin & Van Dyke, Dry Goods. CITY HALL. Northwestern Fuel Co. Dr. A. F. Elliott, Surgeon and Physician. J. S. MARTIN, DRUGGIST.

trong. Credit lines on the print indicate that the work was produced by the
Monasch Company. Among the names of merchants and other occupants are
many names which will be remembered today.

Metropolitan Theatre and Pence Opera House

Gas Light and Grease Paint

Our Minneapolis Theaters

Even as a raw frontier village, hundreds of miles from the nearest railroad, Minneapolis had a hankering for the theater and what was then called "entertainments." Woodman's Hall, opened the year after the city was born, at Washington and Second Avenues South, was the first place of public entertainment, although strictly speaking it was hardly a theater.

Harmonia Hall, first of that name, was built a short time later at Second Avenue North and Second Street, and "musicals" and "entertainments" were given there, too. Then, in 1867, the Pence Opera House was finished at Hennepin Avenue and Second Street, and the city was in business as a theater-going town.

Money from lumbering and the rapidly developing milling industry brought more and more people to the city, increasing demands for all kinds of public recreation. In 1871, the Academy of Music was built at Washington and Hennepin Avenues. This was to be the city's principal theater until 1883.

It was the age of gas light, tall hats and the bustle. If you were fashionable you had a carriage — and when you went to the Academy you left the horses at Eddy's or Parcher's livery stables, or hitched them out front if there was room at the line of hitching posts. You might be going to see the musical extravaganza , "Evangeline," based on Longfellow's poem.

As the Victorian age moved on into ever-increasing opulence, theaters blossomed out all over the rapidly building town. The Theater Comique was opened in 1874, the Standard in 1878, and the old Grand Opera House, on Sixth Street, in 1883. In 1886 Sackett and Wiggins Museum was attracting customers on Hennepin Avenue near Second Street. Two theaters were built in 1887, the Lyceum and the Bijou. The Lyceum Theater opened with an engagement of Booth and Barrett, then among the greatest names in show business.

In 1894, the Metropolitan Opera House, first known as the New People's Theater, went into operation on Marquette Avenue

Interior of People's Theater

between Third and Fourth Streets. For a generation this was to be the center of Minneapolis' theater life.

But the city's desire for a large concert hall, suitable for grand opera and big orchestral concerts, remained unsatisfied until the building of the first Auditorium, now the Lyceum Theater, in 1905. Here the Minneapolis Symphony Orchestra, the Apollo Club and the Philharmonic Club made their appearances.

Meanwhile, vaudeville was reaching its heyday. The old Orpheum, on Seventh Street between Nicollet and Hennepin Avenue, was one of the most popular places in town. The first movie was shown in Minneapolis at the Bijou about 1898. First regularly scheduled motion pictures were at the old Wonderland on Washington Avenue.

Although the Shubert (now the Alvin) was built in 1909, and successfully operated as a stock theater in later years by A. G. "Buzz" Bainbridge, one time mayor, the trend of the entertainment world was already apparent. And the trend was toward movies. Mary Pickford was beginning her career as America's sweetheart. John Bunny was a great favorite. By 1911 there were thirty-two movie houses in Minneapolis. S. L. "Roxy" Rothafel, who was to go on to national fame in the New York theater world, opened the old Lyceum to "pictures." With the characteristic Roxy touch he padded out the bill with an orchestral concert, a forerunner of the spectacular stage shows which were to make his fame.

By 1919 there were sixty-seven movie theaters in Minneapolis, and two years later the first of the "super-colossal" movie theaters, the State, was opened. A wonder for its time, this was advertised as a million-dollar theater. It seated 2,400 persons and was described as "the largest, most elaborate, carefully planned motion picture house between Chicago and the Pacific coast."

The same year the Hennepin Orpheum, with 2,900 seats, also announced as a million-dollar theater, was opened. It replaced the old Seventh Street Orpheum. At the time, the Hennepin Orpheum was the second largest vaudeville theater in the country, outranked only by Loew's State in New York City. In 1927, the Minnesota—now Radio City—was opened. It cost $2,000,000 and was the show place of the entire Upper Midwest.

69

Our Park System...how it grew

Although Minneapolis today has a national reputation for its park system, the founding fathers had difficulty selling the idea in the beginning.

"What do we need with parks?" was the attitude. "There will never be a house south of Tenth Street, and everything beyond is one big park."

Minneapolis' first park was established in 1857 by a grant of three and one-third acres from Edward Murphy, who platted Murphy's addition, at Twenty-second Avenue South and Seven and One-half Street. For years the land was used as a cow pasture. In 1873 the city council appropriated $500 for a fence and a row of trees around the park. Murphy had the work done and the council ordered payment. But the mayor refused to sign the warrant and Murphy never got his money.

In 1883, the Minnesota legislature passed a park bill which was ratified by Minneapolis voters in a city election later that year. On April 27, 1883, the council transferred to the Board of Park Commissioners all park properties then in existence — Murphy Square, Franklin Steele Square, Hawthorne (now Wilson) Park, and Market Square.

C. M. Loring, known as "the father of the park system," was elected first presi-

70

You took your fiddle along when you went rowing on the city lakes back in the Gay Nineties (see opposite page). Women golfers enjoyed the game long before the days of Patty Berg. Today horseback riding and sailing is the vogue in the city of lakes and playgrounds.

At left, a modern concrete bridge spans the Mississippi River to connect the parks and boulevards of Minneapolis. Below at left, one of the many swimming beaches that are under the supervision of the Park Board. Below, the pool and stage of the summer productions of the famous Aqua Follies.

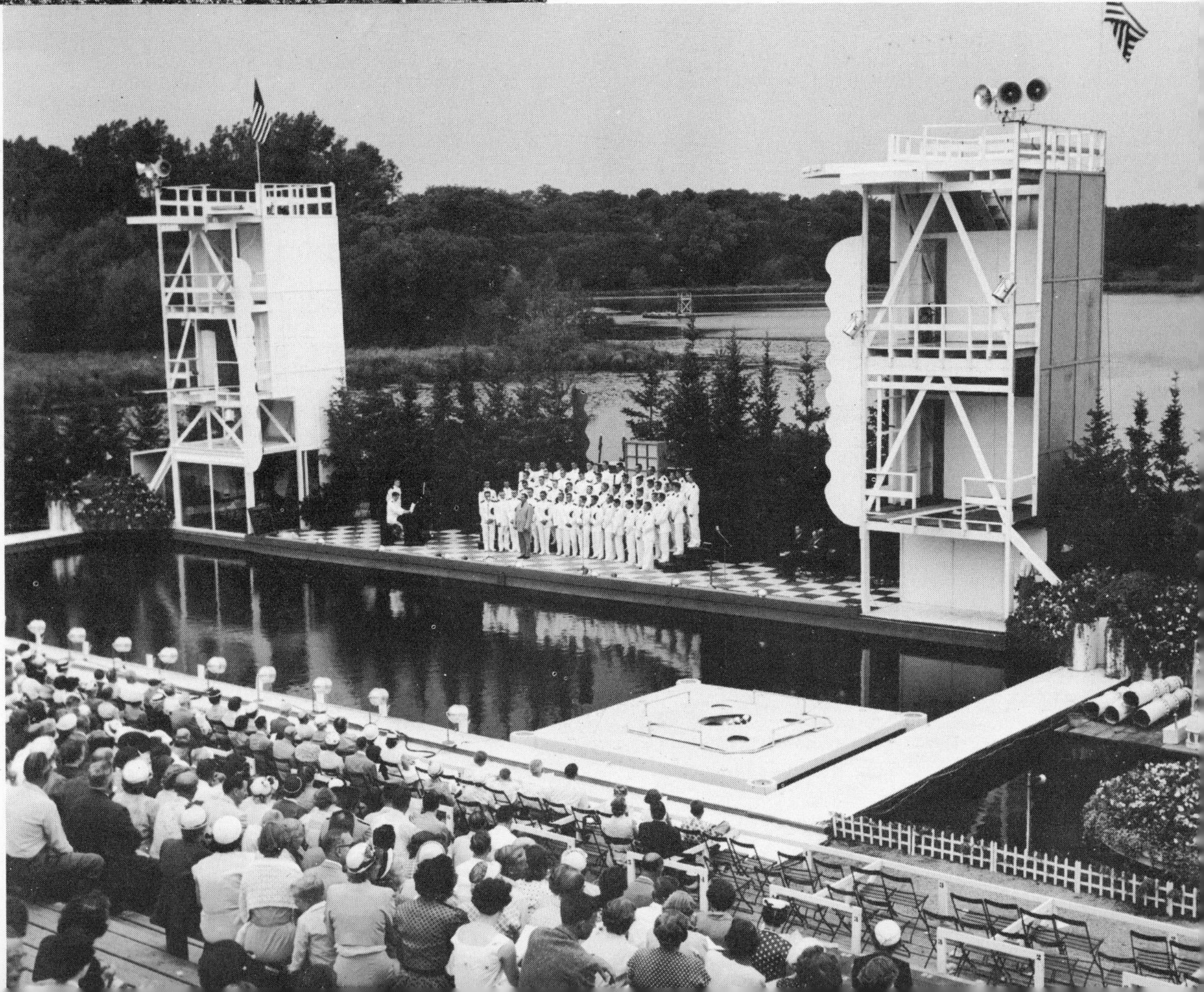

C. M. Loring

Col. Wm. S. King

School children pulling the Stevens House to Minnehaha Park where it was placed in a permanent location.

dent of the park board. H. W. S. Cleveland, expert landscape architect, was engaged to advise the board in planning its work. Colonel W. S. King, pioneer Minneapolis newspaper publisher and one of the founders of the Tribune, came on the board in 1885, and gave large tracts of land around Lake Harriet for the park system. Twenty acres of Sixth Ward Park—now Riverside —along the Mississippi River were bought for $58,500. More properties were added — Loring Park, about 30 acres (called Central Park at the time), Logan Park, Fairview. In the first year of its existence the board purchased 80 acres to add to the six it had inherited from the city council.

From meager beginnings in 1883, the city's park system has been steadily expanded until today it contains 5,897.74 acres, including 22 lakes, with a water area of 1,321 acres; 63 miles of parkways almost completely encircling the city, and 59 playgrounds which are a daily source of recreation for young and old alike.

In the 73 years since the park board was established, the popular concept of the use of parks has been wholly changed. In early times, a park was a place of rest and relaxation with floral displays and well-kept lawns bearing "Keep Off the Grass" signs. Today, the park or playground is a place of teeming activity where citizens, young and old alike, find surcease from the stresses and strains of modern life.

Caleb Dorr and other Hennepin County territorial pioneers plant a group of elms in Loring Park to honor Charles M. Loring, father of Minneapolis parks.

The Growth of the Institute of Arts

Tenth Street. A picture gallery was installed and an art school was opened.

Meanwhile, society members felt a growing need for a building of their own. The World Columbian Exposition in Chicago in 1893, with its galleries of Oriental and American art and its emphasis on neo-classic architecture, stimulated interest in art all over the country. The panic of 1893 struck, however, and the Society of Fine Arts was forced, by economic circumstances, to postpone its building plans.

By 1909, when Edwin Hewitt was president and Eugene Carpenter was vice president, the society was again ready to move forward with building plans. On January 11, 1911, a now historic dinner was given which Dr. Edward Robinson, then director of the Metropolitan Museum in New York, called "one of the classic pages in the history of art."

Clinton Morrison, who had come to Minneapolis in 1855 when he was thirteen years old and who had made his fortune here, donated the land fronting on East Twenty-fourth Street where the Institute

In 1883, seventeen years after the incorporation of Minneapolis, the Minneapolis Society of Fine Arts was founded by a group of twenty-four citizens interested in the cultural opportunities and future of the young city.

In its early days the society had headquarters on Washington Avenue. When the library was opened in 1889 it moved to the new building at Hennepin Avenue and

of Art now stands. Morrison's gift was immediately followed by a $100,000 contribution from William Hood Dunwoody. Within an hour and a half, the society had sixty-seven on-the-spot pledges totaling $335,500. Three years later, Mr. Dunwoody left a $1,000,000 fund for the purchase of works of art, the largest gift in the society's seventy-three-year history.

The institute building was completed in January, 1915. Although it had only about 800 art objects at that time, more than 125,000 people visited the institute in its first eight months. In the forty-one years that have followed, the society never has lost sight of the principle of steady growth. Today, collections total more than 26,000

objects, covering the history of art from 3000 B.C. to the present, an art treasure whose value is more than $10,000,000.

The society's collections have grown through gifts and the establishment of important funds, such as the William Hood Dunwoody fund, the John R. Van Derlip fund, the Ethel Morrison Van Derlip fund and the Lillian Zenobia Turnblad fund.

Some outstanding gifts were received from Herschel V. Jones, Carl W. Jones, Mrs. Charles J. Martin, Mrs. Folwell Coan, Mrs. Eugene Carpenter, Mr. and Mrs. Augustus L. Searle, Alfred F. Pillsbury, Mrs. Charles S. Pillsbury, Mrs. C. C. Webber, Mrs. Clara Hill Lindley, Charles L. Freer, Edward S. Harkness, Miss Lily Place, John D. Rockefeller, Jr., and Chester Dale.

T. B. Walker

and His Legacy of Art

T. B. Walker

Minneapolis' Walker Art Center is one of the largest privately endowed art museums in the United States. It had its origin in the personal art collection of Thomas B. Walker, pioneer lumberman. Walker arrived in Minneapolis in 1862, when he was 22 years old. He came up the Mississippi River on a steam packet of the old Diamond Joe Line and crossed the ten miles between St. Paul and St. Anthony on the first little train. He walked across the old suspension bridge into Minneapolis.

As he prospered, the lumberman began to buy art. His first purchases were modest chromos and engravings. Then, in 1874, he bought his first important painting, a monk by Tambourini. He began buying pottery, porcelains and jades around 1881. His jade collection, one of the finest in the world, was started by a chance purchase at Tiffany's, in New York. Gem glass, necklaces and other jewelry from ancient tombs in Syria, Egypt, and Babylonia, bronze and gold idols from ancient temples in China were bought at sales of private collections in this country and Europe.

Walker's gallery was first in his home on Eighth Street and Hennepin Avenue, now the site of the State theater. In 1879 the lumberman opened his home to the public with 20 paintings on display. Soon 14 rooms were thrown open to visitors and Mrs. Walker engaged an additional maid to answer the door and direct the public.

In 1918 Walker purchased the property on Lowry hill where Walker Art Center is now situated. His plan was to turn 3½ acres over to Minneapolis on which the city was

803 Hennepin Avenue

to erect a library with space for his art collection. There was a lack of interest in the proposal at the time and Walker went ahead on his own. The present building was opened in May, 1927, just a few months before his death.

In 1939 the Walker Art Galleries were renamed the Walker Art Center to signal a reorganization which provided for active programs in education and temporary exhibitions and included plans to add American works, primarily contemporary, to the permanent collection. The first continuous museum program it designed was launched with the Everyday Art Gallery and the publication of the Everyday Art Quarterly, now with an international circulation. In the next few years outstanding works by Lyonel Feininger, Louis Bouche, Asher B. Durand, Albert Ryder, Thomas Eakins and others were acquired.

In recent years added emphasis has been given to contemporary art while still continuing the essential aspects of a museum. Walker Art Center now takes an active interest in not only regional and national work, but in representative contemporary European artists. Some of the recent important acquisitions include paintings of Stuart Davis, Marsden Hartley, Hans Hofmann, Yasuo Kuniyoshi, Fernand Leger, Franz Marc and Georgia O'Keefe, and sculpture by Jean Arp, Alexander Calder, Gaston Lachaise, Gerhard Marcks, Elie Nadelman, Renoir and Rodin.

A program of correlated Twentieth Cen-

Gallery of Everyday Art — Below, Gallery of Paintings

tury arts, including music, drama, theater and the dance, was instituted several years ago with the organization of the Center Arts Council, a volunteer group of local business and professional men and women. One of the outstanding sales and rentals programs of original art was organized and is maintained by the council to aid contemporary artists and to encourage local collectors in the purchase of good art works for their homes. Attendance at the center is now more than 150,000 a year.

W. M. Brackett, organizer

Lumberjack Shirts to Radio Trucks

The Fire Department

U p to 1854, Al Stones's fire company—which meant every able-bodied man in the village armed with a bucket — was the only fire protection in St. Anthony. Then on December 1, 1854, twenty young men of the village organized Cataract Engine Co. No. 1, the first fire engine company in Minnesota territory.

On parade, Cataract No. 1 cut quite a swath — red flannel shirts with blue collars and cuffs, white duck pantaloons with black stripes, and highly glazed caps with the name of the company in gilt on the front.

Minnehaha Hook and Ladder Company was organized in 1857, and Germania Engine Company in 1858. Meanwhile, there was another outfit in town — the Independent Hook and Ladder Company of St. Anthony — which disputed all comers in its claims to priority. Down to the death of the last of them, the old Independents

argued that they were the original fire fighters of Minneapolis.

On July 1, 1879, the Minneapolis Volunteer Fire Department held its last parade. Afterwards, drawn up before the old City Hall on Bridge Square, the 304 members were formally disbanded. By 1885 Minneapolis had a full-time, full-pay fire department of 105 members.

On August 19, 1893, the new full-time department got its first big "baptism of fire"— the worst blaze in the city's history up to that date and still, from the viewpoint of area involved, one of the largest fire disasters in Minneapolis. The panic of 1893 had stacked up huge lumber reserves along the saw mill strip on the river. An unusually long dry period had increased the fire hazards. On a hot Sunday afternoon, with a strong southeast wind blowing, boys started a fire on Nicollet Island. Sparks carried by wind ignited lumber

piles and buildings on Boom Island to the north. The fire jumped the river banks. Before it could be controlled six mills, lumber yards, and more than one hundred houses and buildings over a thirty-block area had been destroyed at a cost of almost one million dollars.

Motorized equipment was first used in the department in 1911. Complete motorization was put through in 1923. On December 24, 1946, the fire department radio system was installed.

Maximum strength of the Minneapolis Fire Department today is 574 men. Of this number, approximately 85 are assigned to headquarters, office, Fire Prevention Bureau, fire alarm system, and repair shop. The remainder are assigned to the department's thirty fire-fighting companies in the city's twenty fire stations. A first-grade fire fighter is paid $435 a month. Reynold C. Malmquist has been chief since 1950.

The first fire truck was purchased in 1858 with 7 ladders, 125 buckets, 9 hooks, and 20 axes. (See pictures of original trucks on this page.) Later the steam engine and horse-drawn truck (opposite page) preceded the use of the modern fire-fighting equipment.

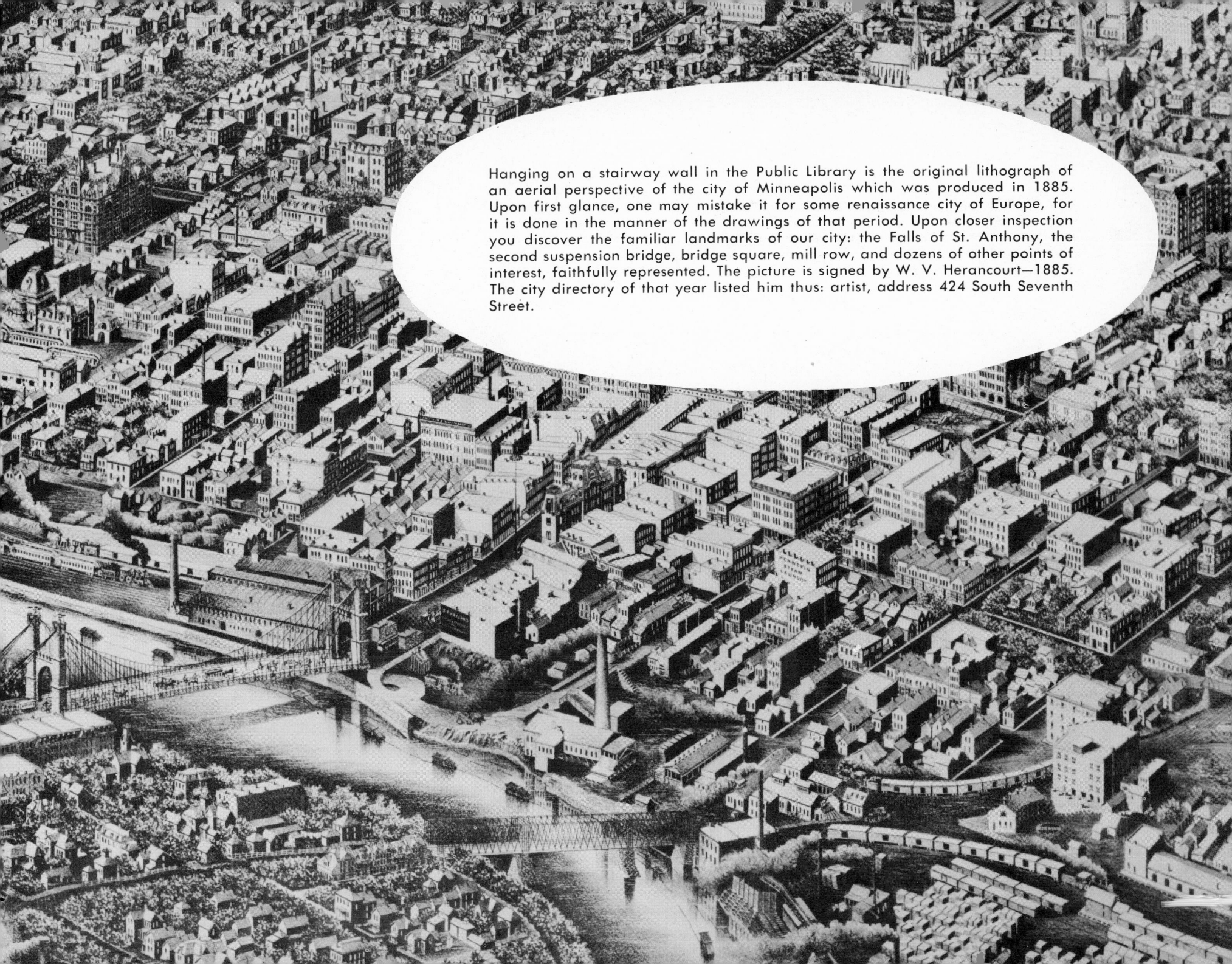

Hanging on a stairway wall in the Public Library is the original lithograph of an aerial perspective of the city of Minneapolis which was produced in 1885. Upon first glance, one may mistake it for some renaissance city of Europe, for it is done in the manner of the drawings of that period. Upon closer inspection you discover the familiar landmarks of our city: the Falls of St. Anthony, the second suspension bridge, bridge square, mill row, and dozens of other points of interest, faithfully represented. The picture is signed by W. V. Herancourt—1885. The city directory of that year listed him thus: artist, address 424 South Seventh Street.

Tribute to City Planners' Foresight

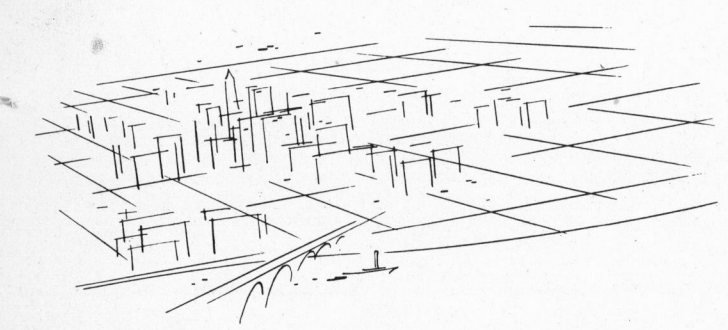

View Minneapolis from the air . . . or from the ground . . . and you appreciate the foresight of city planners who carefully and sensibly plotted broad straight streets long before the coming of the automobile . . . who imposed restrictions on building heights (removed only in recent years) to stimulate a wider spread, less confusing downtown area . . . who realized that beauty and business need not be widely separated . . . it's only a ten minute walk from the center of the "loop" to beautiful Loring Park, only a ten minute ride to Lake Harriet, Lake Calhoun, or Lake of the Isles.

The Growth of Retail Trade

Like many other things in Minneapolis, the great department stores and fine specialty shops that today line Nicollet Avenue can trace their business descent back to Fort Snelling and the fur trade.

Franklin Steele's sutler's store at the army post was the first retail establishment in the area and in the late 1840's the great fur trading firm of Pierre Chouteau & Company of St. Louis opened a branch in St. Anthony.

As early as 1847 Roswell P. Russell had a little shop in the Luther Patch house in St. Anthony. In 1851 John H. Stevens and Franklin Steele opened a general store, and in 1853 Thomas Chambers leased a building from Colonel Stevens near the ferry for the first store on the west side of the river.

For years, the frontier lived on the "general store." It was not until later that the big department stores developed. G. W. Hale & Company began business in 1867 and this was to evolve over the years into J. W. Thomas & Company.

In 1878 Goodfellow & Eastman opened a store on Nicollet Avenue near Washington. George D. Dayton of Worthington, Minnesota, later acquired R. S. Goodfellow & Company, successor to Goodfellow & Eastman, and this was the beginning of the great department store, The Dayton Compay, now known from coast to coast.

Powers grew out of S. E. Olson & Company which for years was known as "The Big Store." William and L. S. Donaldson purchased Colton & Company, known as "the Glass Block Store," in 1884, and this was the beginning of Donaldson's.

Minneapolis retail stores today have a justly deserved reputation for being among the most beautiful and progressive in the nation. In recent years there has been a trend towards establishing branches in the suburbs. As Minneapolis expands, its downtown retail business is expanding with it.

Nicollet Avenue, 1956

In 1869, the first Chamber of Commerce good-will tour was made by wagon and horseback as far west as the Missouri River. At left is shown the return of the caravan to Minneapolis after a two months' trip.

NICOLLET AVE. of many years ago.

NICOLLET AVE. of today.

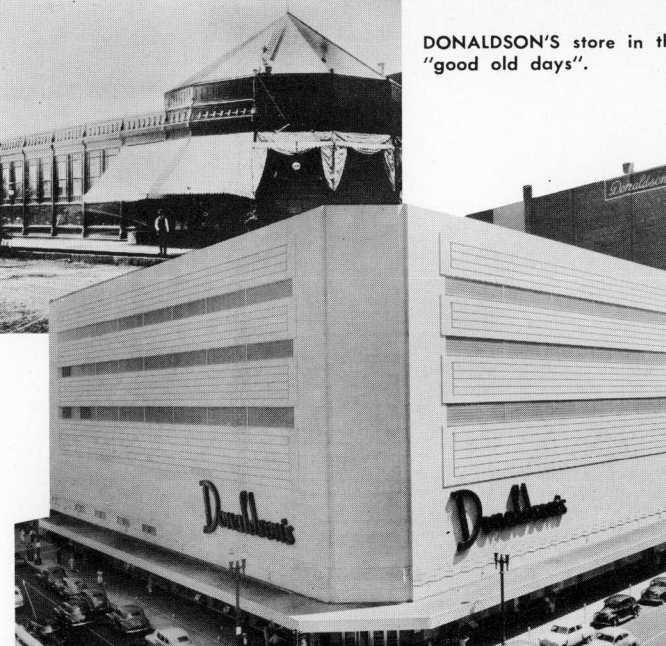

DONALDSON'S store in the "good old days".

GROWING . . .

SIDE BY SIDE

MINNEAPOLIS AND *Donaldson's*

BETWEEN 6th AND 7th ON NICOLLET

Partner's in progress . . . Donaldson's and Minneapolis. Minneapolis, founded 100 years ago, now a great and important center in the upper midwest. Donaldson's founded 75 years ago, the first department store in the entire Northwest. The growth of a store is intertwined with the growth of a city. As we observe our 75th Anniversary, it's interesting to contrast the old with new . . . . the changes that have so altered the face of our city as well as our store.

Side by side we have grown . . . and shall continue to grow . . . ever enlarging our facilities and ever increasing our services to people of Minneapolis and the Upper Midwest. To keep growing with Minneapolis we dedicate ourselves to a program of keeping faith with our customers with the policies they have approved during the past 75 years, the same policies that have been responsible for Donaldson's being a partner in progress with Minneapolis during the years.

Everybody enjoys shopping in Everybody's Store

F. W. WOOLWORTH COMPANY

The freedom to choose from a great variety of goods to meet the needs of modern living, all in open display, all plainly priced—this freedom of self-selection is one of the greatest boons today's shopper owes to the pioneering of F. W. Woolworth and his Co-Founders. Today Woolworths brings the pleasurable profitable adventure of modern shopping to every member of every family in many communities.

Woolworth Stores are essentially local stores that help build the community and contribute to its prosperity.

Woolworths is proud of its 52 years of citizenship in Minneapolis, and joins with pride in the city's 100th birthday celebration.

1879

F. W. Woolworth, founder of the Woolworth stores, lived in the era of the horse-car but he planned and built for the future.

In 1917 Liberty Bond Drives were conducted all over America. Nicollet Avenue in Minneapolis was the scene of many sales demonstrations as illustrated by the picture above. Below is a picture of the famous Sky Room of Dayton's that is one of the attractions in Minneapolis.

Another milestone in the growth of Minneapolis

Southdale Center, 1956

We are proud that Dayton's great new suburban shopping development, Southdale Center, will open in 1956, Minneapolis Centennial Year, giving added proof of the growth of our city and inaugurating a new era in shopping comfort and convenience for us all.

Dayton's

We've been growing with Minneapolis for over seventy years

The first store in Minneapolis with electric lights . . the first complete men's store . . the first fashion specialty store in the United States . . the first to bring imports to the Northwest . . the first store in America with its own auto ramp—these are but a few of the many, many firsts of a store that's been a visitor's mecca almost as long as Minnehaha Falls. A store which has always made a fetish of fashion . . whose names stand for quality that's unqualified, for satisfaction that's guaranteed.

We've grown, built and expanded with Minneapolis . . and the hopes, aims, traditions of our founders have always been our guideposts . . *and always will be!*

Maurice L Rothschild
Young-Quinlan Co

The Way We Lived Then - III

Interior, Residence of F. C. Pillsbury

They called them "the Elegant Eighties" —the high-hatted, frock-coated, horse-drawn years between the governorships of John S. Pillsbury and William R. Merriam. It was an age when bearded men in long black coats addressed each other in formal, decorous language, when ladies had afternoons "at home" and the mark of worldly success was a well-polished carriage, with gleaming brasswork, shiny leather, handsome horses and a coachman.

Minneapolis had spread out from its pioneer days, but in the light of modern suburban development most of the 1880 city seems almost "down town." Seventh Street and Sixth Avenue South was one of the best residential areas. So was Nicollet Island. Grove Place was filled with fine, old-fashioned homes. The DeLaittres, the Nimrocks, the Eastmans, the Eustises, and the Charles A. Heffelfingers still lived on the Island.

Far out, toward the University on Fifth Street Southeast, was the elegant home of

Governor Pillsbury, with its porte-cochere, elaborate woodwork, little window balconies and towering chimneys—one of the show places of the city. Refinished and modernized, it is now the residence of the president of the University of Minnesota.

Franklin Avenue was the city limits. Lowry hill was only sparsely settled. Park Avenue was a swank residential area but there were few houses beyond Twenty-third Street. Third Avenue South, out as far as the present Art Institute, was one of the choice places to live. Fair Oaks, the W. D. Washburn mansion, took in more than a block between Third and Stevens Avenues, Twenty-first and Twenty-fourth Streets.

If the Eighties were elegant, they also were fussy and uncomfortable. It was a time when little girls wore fluffy white frocks, when brides went to the altar preceded by horns of plenty filled with pink and white carnations. Women wore three petticoats under heavy and elaborate dresses, and men were strait-jacketed in boiled shirts, high

minneapolis was only twenty-five—

It was 1881. Boardwalks were the "latest thing." Paved streets were no more than a gleam in the "visionary's" eye. Washington Avenue was our main business street, and the site where the auditorium was later built was almost "suburban." That's how it was when Powers was born, 75 years ago, when Minneapolis was only 25. Since that time we've *both* grown and prospered. Our destinies are twined together. So it is that we at Powers salute you, Minneapolis, and the men and women who gave you life. May your future be as brilliant as your past!

Powers

MINNEAPOLIS-KNOLLWOOD

POWERS · DIAMOND · JUBILEE ·

When it comes to smart fashions...

it's *John W. Thomas & Co.*

NICOLLET AT EIGHTH

for over eighty-seven years, the store

chosen by five generations of young

fashion-alert customers.

stiff collars and detachable "hard" cuffs.

It was an age that yearned for culture. It read Ralph Waldo Emerson's "Good Manners" and tried to be guided by the standards of Boston and New York drawing rooms. It was highly improper to smoke in the presence of ladies, and smoking on the street was the sign of the boor.

It was the age of the formal note and the calling card. Every home with any pretension to culture had a table in the front hall bearing a silver tray, or other receptacle, in which visitors were expected to leave engraved cards according to a rigid social formula.

It was the age of the polka and the waltz —and Prof. Danz' orchestra. All maidens were shy, all swains bashful. Relations between boys and girls were supposed to be highly formal and the chaperone was a fixed feature of society. It was an age when the overgrown country town, a frontier outpost twenty years before, was trying desperately to be a city—and, in a measure and according to prevailing lights, succeeding.

Business Property
Specialists
SINCE 1881

J. F. Conklin

J. F. CONKLIN, pioneer among realtors of Minneapolis, began his business in 1881. Among his first assignments was the management of the Old Grand Opera House. Since those early days, management of business properties has been a specialty of this firm now in its seventy-fifth year. These services have included leasing and operating of properties, mortgage loans, insurance, brokerage and appraisals.

TODAY — Conklin-Zonne-Loomis Company is under the supervision of E. Herrick Conklin, son of its founder, and R. A. Price, who has been associated with the firm for nineteen years. The company manages more than thirty buildings and estates in metropolitan Minneapolis, passing on to its clientele the benefits of its many years of specialized experience.

CONKLIN-ZONNE-LOOMIS
COMPANY • *REALTORS*

701 First National-Soo Line Bldg.
Minneapolis, Minnesota

From our early files

- Real Estate
- Property Management
- Mortgage Loans
- Insurance
- Rentals
- Appraisals

94

One of the bright spots for recreation and promenading on a Sunday afternoon was around the Lake Harriet Pavilion.

A group of fashionable young people in 1905 waiting to board an excursion train for a jaunt out to Lake Minnetonka.

84 years IN MINNEAPOLIS

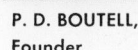

P. D. BOUTELL,
Founder

Boutells joins the city of Minneapolis in celebration — the 100th Anniversary for the City, the 84th birthday for Boutells. This notable occasion will be highlited for Boutells by the opening of its first Suburban Branch in Southdale — one of the nation's largest, most modern, retail shopping districts.

Since that day in 1872 when Founder, P. D. Boutell, opened his furniture store on Washington Avenue, Boutells has been an integral part of Minneapolis' business community, and today has arrived at the stature of being one of the most complete and most important home furnishing stores in the entire country. Boutells has built their reputation on fashion — wise home furnishings of dependable quality and nationally well-known names and brands. Boutells is proud of its reputation and business policies and the fact that many thousands of families have been customers for three generations. In addition to complete furnishings for the home, Boutells caters to hospitals, hotels, universities, city schools and similar institutions. Boutells interior decorating studio is staffed to accommodate all decorating tasks, whether large or small, Boutells proudly joins our great city in this anniversary — and looks forward to the privilege of serving its citizens in this ever expanding area in the fine State of Minnesota.

Southdale

Boutells

MARQUETTE AT FIFTH STREET
MINNEAPOLIS, 2, MINNESOTA

HEARTIEST GOOD WISHES, MINNEAPOLIS!

... J. C. PENNEY

Mr. A. L. Remington
J. C. Penney Company
Minneapolis, Minn.

**First Penney store
opened in Kemmerer,
Wyoming, 1902**

Dear Al:

Thanks for reminding me that this is Centennial Year for Minneapolis. Please extend my heartiest good wishes to all the people of your fine city. They have accepted us as neighbors for 20 years now: our services have expanded, so they evidently consider us good neighbors.

You were no more than a boy, Al, when the first Penney store opened in Minneapolis; but there still are a good many of us who remember the occasion well. It was in 1936, and business was "a little better" than it had been; but not much, I'm afraid. We were very proud to be opening a store in Minneapolis, though, and we all said Minneapolis has a "future."

Today, our faith in Minneapolis projects itself into the city's second century of development. I am not only pleased about that but deeply impressed, as well. Plans to expand your present modern store are being studied now, as you know. I am sure you will agree with me that those plans are the best possible evidence that the Penney Company will do its best to keep step with the greater Minneapolis that is going to develop during the city's second hundred years.

With kindest personal regards, I am

Very truly yours,

J. C. Penney

**Proposed Penney
store for
Minneapolis, 1958**

Horse Car to Motor Bus

By the end of the Civil War, the growing young city was beginning to feel the need for public transportation. In 1867 a group which included Dorilus Morrison, B. S. Bull, William S. Judd, Frederick A. Gilson and Godfrey Sheitlin, tried to launch a street railway system and actually got a franchise. But they were a little in advance of their time and it was not until 1873 that things began to move.

In that year a young, ambitious lawyer from Illinois, Thomas Lowry, became interested in the street car project. With eight other men he raised $250,000 in working capital and the Minneapolis Street Railway Company was formed. The City Council granted a franchise in 1875 and the first car with a full load of passengers moved on September 2, 1875.

The early horsecars weighed about 1,000 pounds, accommodated fourteen persons, and were drawn by a single horse. Passengers sat facing each other on two long seats running the length of the car. There was a small iron stove in the center, a smelly oil lamp, and about a foot of hay on the floor to keep passengers' feet warm in cold weather.

In 1875 the city had 4.37 miles of track. Five years later this had grown to nine miles and the company was extending its trackage every year. Twelve miles of new track were laid in 1883 alone. And by 1884, so successful was the venture, that

Lowry and his group were ready to take over the St. Paul system and make the two a Twin City organization.

It was recognized early that horse cars soon would be inadequate for the rapidly growing city. In the late 1870's and 1880's there were attempts to operate steam locomotive lines. Then Lowry learned of the success of Thomas A. Edison and Stephen D. Field in developing the electric trolley. In 1889 the first electric cars were in operation in Minneapolis.

Electrification was pushed rapidly. New equipment was purchased. Heavier rails were installed. The old narrow gauge

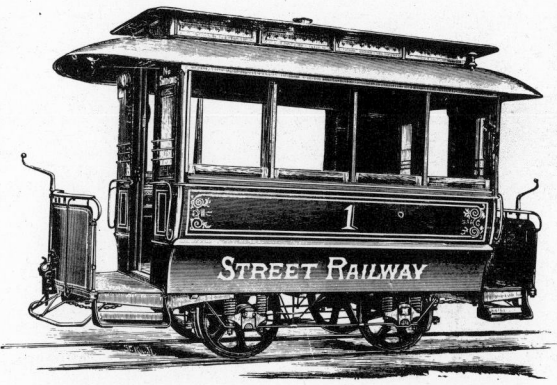

In 1890, The Northern Car Company was building ten cars (above) a week which were sold nationwide. In 1888, the horse drawn streetcar was the latest type of transportation in Minneapolis.

97

Horse Car to Motor Bus

horse-car lines were junked and standard gauge tracks were built all over the two cities. It was the era of the streetcar and things were booming. The lines were expanded to the Minnetonka area on the west and to White Bear and Stillwater on the east.

In 1922 the Twin City Rapid Transit Company carried 226,000,000 passengers — but even then the "acids of modernity" were at work, changing transportation systems even as they were changing all other phases of American life. The booming automobile industry, shifts in population and the rise of the suburbs were bringing different living habits, different patterns of movement among people. Ten years after the 1922 peak the company collected only 113,000,000 fares and by 1940 the total was down to 104,000,000. It was

plain that the old-time streetcar was in trouble.

In the late 1940's, the company purchased a large fleet of new streetcars in an effort to revive the business. But by 1951 it was apparent that this was not good enough. Some lines were operating at 60 and 65 cents a mile costs, but collecting only 16 to 20 cents a mile revenue. Charles Green, a New York financier, assumed the presidency of the company in 1949 and began to lop off lines that did not pay.

About a year after gaining control of the company, Green sold out. A short time later Fred A. Ossanna, Minneapolis attorney who had been legal counsel for the company, took over and immediately launched plans to put Twin City Lines back on its feet.

Ossanna quickly saw that conversion to buses must be put through immediately to insure survival of the system. Arrangements were made to purchase 525 new diesel buses from General Motors Corporation. Today, the company operates 880 buses and last year carried 81,294,859 passengers a total of 23,300,744 miles. The company has 1,641 employes.

Transportation methods change rapidly in a growing city. New buses have replaced streetcars and modern automobiles have replaced the electric broughams of 1905.

Typical horse-car used in 1872, when Twin City Lines was first formed. The system consisted of 30 horses, fifteen cars and 14 drivers, with receipts averaging about $50.00 a day.

1872 ... 1956

Some of the new General Motors Air-Suspension, 51 passenger, diesel buses, now serving the Twin Cities. Over 875 now adorn the streets of our two great cities.

TWIN CITY LINES and MINNEAPOLIS HAVE GROWN TOGETHER

In 1872, Twin City Lines began its operation of public transportation in Minneapolis. From that time until now, it has grown and is progressive and forward-looking . . . like Minneapolis itself.

In 1952, we began our conversion from streetcars to buses with our main objective, to make this system the finest in the country. In less than 25 months, we were able to transform a sprawling, confused system, into a modern engineered network, served by the world's largest fleet of new 51-passenger, air ride, diesel buses. This was accomplished in four years less time than outside experts predicted as a possibility.

Today, Twin City Lines proudly boasts one of the most modern and finest transportation systems, not only in the country, but in the WORLD. Over 875 buses, 525 of the very latest design, and 1,100 well-trained operators are at your service, giving you, our customers, the finest, safest and most economical transportation available.

We are proud of our responsibility to supply the public transportation needs of Minneapolis. This company has at all times tried to keep abreast of the needs of this growing metropolis. With the cooperation of the people and its public officials, our city will continue to prosper and our company enabled to meet its requirements.

"Public transit is still the most vital force in the growth and life of this community. Better public understanding of its problems will help create a finer service."

TWIN CITY LINES

SERVICE
COURTESY
SAFETY

The wood carvings made by Warren T. Mosman for the lobby of the Farmers and Mechanics Savings Bank symbolize the basic natural resources behind Minneapolis progress.

Banking was built upon resources

The frontier was the great stamping grounds of the jack-of-all-trades — and frontier bankers were likely to buy and sell almost anything. Loans and deposits were only part of their business. Insurance, real estate, brokerage and wholesaling were all mixed up in frontier banking.

In 1857 Jacob K. Sidle of York, Pennsylvania, arrived in Minneapolis and with Peter Wolford and $10,000 opened an office on Hennepin Avenue labeled "Sidle, Wolford and Company." In 1864, the Sidle company became the Minneapolis Bank and in 1865 this, in turn, became the First National Bank of Minneapolis.

Lumbermen and flour millers were prominent in the organization of the Northwestern National Bank in 1872. Dorilus Morrison, the first mayor, was elected president, and William Hood Dunwoody was the first depositor. In 1874 the Farmers and Mechanics Savings Bank was organized by Clinton Morrison, son of Dorilus Morrison, and E. H. Moulton.

Since those early days, the First National Bank and the Northwestern National Bank have grown into banking giants. Total resources of each of the "big banks," today is more than four hundred million dollars. In all, there are nineteen banks within the Minneapolis city limits, and thirty-one banks in Minneapolis and the immediate suburbs.

FORECASTING ANOTHER 100 YEARS OF PROGRESS FOR MINNEAPOLIS

They say the first 100 years are the hardest. That may be so . . . but they're the most satisfying, too! ❧ *For 84 of those 100 years here at Northwestern Bank, we've been building and growing along with our city. And we've enjoyed every day of it!* ❧ *A look to the past brings back pleasant memories of happy associations with the city and with a good share of the people who have lived in and around it.* ❧ *And just as our weatherball signs forecast the weather, so a look to the future leads us to forecast that the next 100 years will be as full of accomplishment.*

HAPPY CENTURY TO A GRAND TOWN!

Northwestern Banks of the Minneapolis Area

Growing with the Northwest . . . helping the Northwest grow.

After a century of change...SAVING IS STILL IN STYLE

19th Century mechanical coin bank

Grandfather's wondrous mechanical bank may be a museum piece today, but in this thrifty city, saving has always *stayed* in style.

No one knows it better than Farmers & Mechanics. For more than 81 years we've watched this thriving young mill town grow—and watched our family of depositors grow steadily along with it.

Today, in Minneapolis' only mutual savings bank, we safeguard some 210,000 accounts. That's an average of more than one account for every home in this town—including a good many homes F & M home loans have financed!

With savings deposits now at an all-time high, our city has built a firm foundation for future growth. We're looking forward to Minneapolis' *next* 100 years—and to greater growth still to come.

Farmers & Mechanics

SAVINGS BANK OF MINNEAPOLIS

MEMBER FEDERAL DEPOSIT INSURANCE CORPORATION

1857

North Side of
Hennepin Avenue
opposite Bridge Square

1858

Old Nicollet
House, Washing-
ton at Hennepin

1864

N. W. Corner of Nicollet
Avenue and Washington
— now part of Gateway Park

1907

5th at Marquette

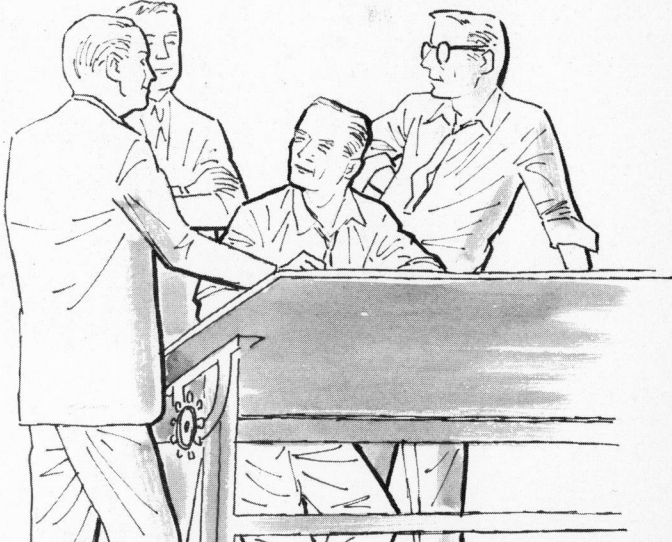

TODAY
5th at Marquette

The FIRST *hundred years . . .*

During this our own 100th year, First National Bank salutes the City of Minneapolis on its Centennial . . .

Since our founding in 1857, as a private bank headed by J. K. Sidle, there have been many striking parallels in the growth of the Bank and the community we are privileged to serve. Those men who built First National to its present position are men who also made a significant contribution to the development of Minneapolis. Theirs, through the years, has been the staunch belief that the Bank, as a strong financial friend of the community, should serve its people sincerely and progressively.

It is to this principle that First National stands dedicated as we move ahead with Minneapolis into what is for both of us our second century of achievement . . .

☆　☆　AND　TOMORROW　☆　☆　☆　☆

Our new multi-million dollar building . . . now on the drafting boards . . . will occupy most of the block in which we now are situated. It will rise as a symbol of our confidence of the continued growth of Minneapolis and First National Bank.

FIRST NATIONAL BANK

founded in 1857 • *Oldest Bank in Minneapolis*

MEMBER FEDERAL DEPOSIT INSURANCE CORPORATION

Midland Loves Minneapolis

When our bank was born in 1909, our assets were $1,000,000. Today, Midland's assets are over $76,000,000. That's why we love Minneapolis. That's why we add a grateful "thank you" as we congratulate Minneapolis on its 100th birthday. Without Minneapolis' help Midland wouldn't be the city's third largest commercial bank today.

We started small in 1909, when Minneapolis was already a husky growing town, but since then our growth has kept pace with the city. We have much in common—several of our founders were active in aiding the growth of Minneapolis as well as our bank. Among these men were Nils Werner, president of our bank, then known as Scandinavian American National Bank. On the board was Andreas Ueland, father of today's president,

Arnulf Ueland. Others on the board were Eugene Tetzlaff, founder of the Flour City Ornamental Iron Works, Aaron Carlson, pioneer mill work manufacturer, and John Lind, Governor of Minnesota. Under their guidance, Midland was soon to become an integral part of the banking economy and growth of Minneapolis.

The new bank prospered from the start. On the day it opened it acquired the People's bank with deposits of $575,000. In 1910, the Minnesota National Bank was purchased and in later years the bank also bought the National City Bank, Union State Bank and the Sixth Street Bank.

While the purchase of small banks stimulated business for the original bank, it is significant that Midland's greatest growth

has come through new business. Since 1940 when Midland's deposits were $17,000,000 Midland's deposits have increased four-fold. The Scandinavian American National Bank became Midland Bank in 1917 but it retained the policy of friendliness established by the original bank. In recent years extensive modernization has increased the pleasant atmosphere which has become synonymous with "Midland, the bank with the big welcome." The bank is completely air-conditioned, and music is piped into all departments. In the process of modernization is the Midland Bank Building which was acquired in 1953. The opening of an enclosed drive-in bank is scheduled for spring 1956.

Again we say Midland Bank loves Minneapolis. You've been good to us and we thank you!

Eventful Years OF SERVICE

1946 Fort Snelling closed as an Army Post.

1928 K.S.T.P. began first radio broadcasting on March 28th.

1921 State Institution for Savings becomes Marquette Trust Company.

1908 Gateway Park established.

1934 Marquette Bank and Marquette Trust Company affiliated.

1905 Guarantee Savings and Loan Company changes its name to State Institution for Savings.

1889 State of Minnesota grants charter to Guarantee Savings and Loan Company.

1899 Minnesota's 13th Regiment returns from the Phillipine Islands.

1893 Minnesota legislature adopts a state flag.

1955 Marquette National Bank moves to new quarters at Seventh and Marquette.

1924 Memorial Stadium at University of Minnesota dedicated November 15th.

Minneapolis 1856 to 1956

For Minneapolis and the Marquette National Bank, 1956 is a year of special significance.

This year, Minneapolis celebrates a century of spectacular growth . . . the Marquette Bank, its 67th birthday. As Minneapolis has grown, the Marquette Bank has grown with it. Indeed, the growth of one has been inseparably linked with the growth of the other.

When the State of Minnesota granted a charter to the Guarantee Savings and Loan Company in 1889, the city hospital was only a year old, and the Public Library had just opened. Sixteen years later, the Guarantee Savings and Loan Company changed its name to the State Institution for Savings. Then, on July 28th, 1921—the year the last saw-mill in Minneapolis disappeared— the Bank's charter was changed to a trust company organization, and became the Marquette Trust Company. Six months later, the Marquette Bank and Marquette Trust Company were affiliated, and in March, 1934, the two firms were consolidated under the name of the Marquette National Bank of Minneapolis.

During the last decade, the Marquette Bank's continued growth called for more space . . . and on June 18th, 1955, the Bank moved into its new and modern quarters in the Marquette Bank Building, at Seventh Street and Marquette Avenue. Here, in an area almost double the floor-space of its former location, the Bank offers present and future customers every modern facility for making banking convenient, efficient and pleasant.

From this vantage-point, the Marquette Bank extends to Minneapolis hearty congratulations on its first "Century of Progress," and all good wishes for the city's continuing growth and increasing prosperity in the years that lie ahead.

THE MARQUETTE NATIONAL BANK
OF MINNEAPOLIS

MEMBER FEDERAL DEPOSIT INSURANCE CORPORATION

Seventh at Marquette

ONE-THIRD OF A CENTURY OLD

Back in 1923 we opened our doors with little more than dreams and ambition for resources. Today, following one-third of a century of sound, steady growth, we own large, modern, convenient office buildings in downtown Minneapolis and St. Paul. We employ 175 people. Our resources exceed 225 million dollars. We are the largest federal savings and loan association in the United States. To us, growth means an increasing capacity to serve the community and to help more and more people achieve the pleasure and security of home ownership.

Thanks to You

We are sincerely grateful to the thousands upon thousands of savers and borrowers whose confidence and good will have made our progress possible. To all who may wish to use our services, we extend a cordial welcome. Whether you save a few dollars or many thousands, we are happy to serve you. Whether the home you wish to buy is large or small, we are pleased to help you finance it.

TWIN CITY FEDERAL
SAVINGS and LOAN

"Where the TWIN-CLOCK flashes Time and Temperature"

FREE PARKING WHILE YOU TRANSACT BUSINESS

INVESTORS DIVERSIFIED SERVICES, INC., INVESTORS BUILDING, MINNEAPOLIS

Founded in 1894

EXCLUSIVE DISTRIBUTOR AND INVESTMENT MANAGER

FOR MUTUAL FUNDS

INVESTORS MUTUAL, INC.

INVESTORS STOCK FUND, INC.

INVESTORS SELECTIVE FUND, INC.

INVESTORS GROUP CANADIAN FUND LTD.

FOR FACE AMOUNT CERTIFICATES

INVESTORS SYNDICATE OF AMERICA, INC.

Investors DIVERSIFIED SERVICES, INC.

MINNEAPOLIS 2, MINNESOTA

PROSPECTUS UPON REQUEST

From Dog Team to Television

In the winter of 1851 the only contact with the outside world was by dog train. With the invention of the telephone the first line was strung in 1877 from the city hall to the Hankinson residence. Today a daily average of 2,000,000 local phone calls and 37,000 long distance calls, utilizing 4,000 employees, reveals the march of progress in communication. Any civilized place in the world is only a few seconds away from Minneapolis—by phone. In 1892 the American District Telegraph Company was organized in Minneapolis with a capitalization of $15,000. It was the first company to make a success of its fire alarm system. Modern science produced radio and television and today the residents of the Minneapolis area are kept in hourly touch with news events of the world. This is truly the miracle of the past century.

Your Telephone Service Has Come a Long Way . . .

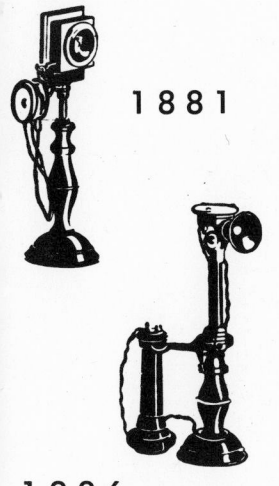

1881

1886

SINCE THAT DAY IN JUNE, 1877, when Richard Henry Hankinson strung Minneapolis' first telephone line between his residence and the old city hall.

Telephone apparatus was crude. The first telephone circuit consisted of a single iron wire with a "wet" battery for power. The first switchboard was made out of old sewing machine parts, and the earliest instruments were box-like affairs that looked like potato mashers.

Today, $82,000,000 worth of equipment gives Minneapolis' 365,000 phones direct, high quality communication with 97% of the world's telephones. Telephone service is furnished to motor vehicles, boats, railroad trains, and airplanes. Modern instruments are available that will answer your incoming calls and take messages when you are away; they can be equipped with microphones and loud speakers so that you can talk without lifting the receiver. They can have light-up dials and adjustable bells.

Truly, your telephone service has come a long way . . . it has grown with Minneapolis. We are confident that this city will continue to prosper in the centennial to come, and we pledge that your telephone system will keep pace with the needs of the city and its people.

NORTHWESTERN BELL TELEPHONE COMPANY

LANDMARKS

Can be New...*

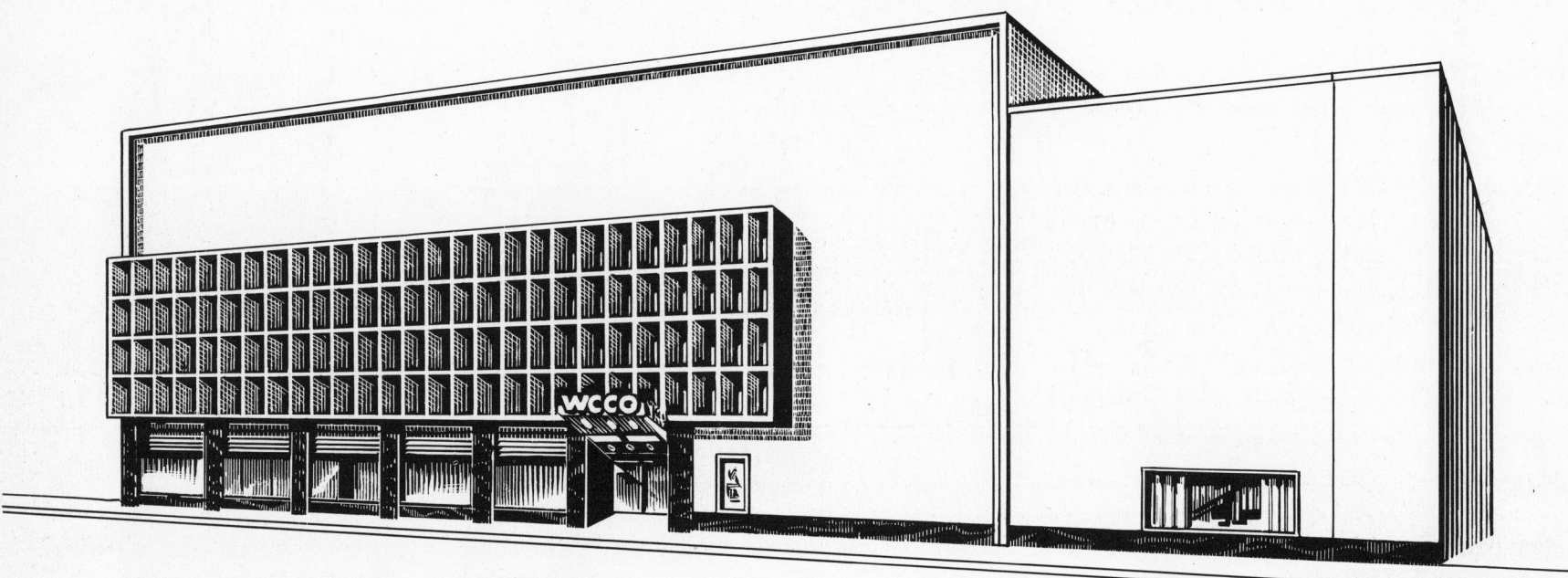

*The new home of WCCO-TV, now under construction

Another Landmark in Over a Half Million Homes

WCCO *television*

CHANNEL 4 • CBS TELEVISION IN THE NORTHWEST

FIRST in the NORTHWEST!

In 1939, KSTP purchased one of the first television cameras in the United States for experimental purposes.

On April 27, 1948, exactly twenty years since KSTP Radio had established itself as a Minneapolis pioneer, television station KSTP-TV began full commercial operation . . . the *first* television station in the Northwest.

Since then, KSTP Radio and TV has added many more *firsts* to its record and has maintained its position as "The Northwest's Leading Station."

Under the leadership of Stanley E. Hubbard, President and General Manager, KSTP will continue to lead the way in the rich, growing market it serves so well.

RADIO **KSTP** TELEVISION

NBC AFFILIATE — MINNEAPOLIS • ST. PAUL

"the northwest's leading station"

REPRESENTED BY EDWARD PETRY & CO., INC.

The showplace of radio-television broadcasting in the Northwest, KSTP Television City is located at 3415 University Avenue. It is the largest independent station in the country, was designed and constructed exclusively for radio and television production. The 600-foot tower is the highest structure in the area.

Indian Trails in 1856 . . .
A Thriving Metropolis A Century Later

High above the diagonal thoroughfare of Hennepin Avenue—once an Indian trail—the airplane passenger sees a panorama of Minneapolis that is startling, as well as beautiful—with its stately buildings and sparkling lakes nestled within its area. When you contrast the present-day view with what the Sioux Indians saw on the trail below in 1856, you are indeed impressed with the courage and foresight of the early pioneers who transformed a wilderness area and laid the foundation for the growth of our north star metropolis. Here is the shining symbol of the lives of devoted men—citizens who built wisely and contributed much to the growth and development of Minneapolis.

Cyrus Northrup

William M. Folwell

The University of Minnesota—
City Within a City

Where the Mississippi River curves south below St. Anthony Falls stands the University of Minnesota on a site selected in 1854. This view from the air shows the main campus with the football stadium in the background. On the opposite page is the Cyrus Northrop Memorial Auditorium.

Incorporated by the territorial legislature of 1851, the University of Minnesota existed, at least on paper, before there was a Minneapolis. Today, the city surrounds the main campus of the university on all sides, and the university has become a vitally important, integral part of Minneapolis.

Time was, in the early years, when the university was "way out in the country." One small building was enough to take care of its needs. Today the university extends for many city blocks over a wide area of southeast Minneapolis.

Speaking of the Minneapolis centennial and the university's relation to the city, President J. L. Morrill has said: "From the beginnings of both, the city and the university have shared problems and prospects. They have been a 'city within a city,' partners in a century of progress."

"Our university people," President Morill continued, "our staff, have been largely citizens of Minneapolis, bound up and active in community affairs. Our activities and expenditures have been a significant factor in community prosperity. The city, its civic and cultural advantages, have pro-

vided a stimulating and attractive climate in which to live and work and grow."

"So it will continue to be as both move forward into a larger destiny," President Morrill predicted. "The outlook is a challenging one to be faced with the same confidence and faith in the future that have brought us to our present high place among the cities and universities of the nation."

The struggling little institution for which City Father Franklin Steele, one of the first regents, advanced money out of his pocket 100 years ago, is today one of the great universities of the world. Its students are drawn not only from the State of Minnesota and the United States but from the farthest corners of the earth. Its work in medicine, surgery, dentistry, agriculture, mining and technology have given it a global stature and reputation. People come from all over the world seeking the benefits of its teaching and its research.

Today the University of Minnesota is the second or third largest university in the nation — depending on how enrollment figures are taken. (College and university size ratings vary according to the methods used in compiling enrollment figures.) More than 23,000 students today attend the University of Minnesota. It has a faculty of 4,170 persons. Last year its payroll was in excess of $30,000,000.

In the long list of Minneapolis' outstanding assets the University has won, and deserves, the place at the top.

In this test-tube above—from the Chemical Engineering Building—may well come the discovery that will start an entire new industry. At the right is Coffman Memorial Union, the student's building dedicated to that important phase of learning—how to get along with your fellow man.

The Minneapolis Symphony plays to enthusiastic thousands during regular concert seasons in Northrop Memorial Auditorium. Basketball is a major sports attraction in Minneapolis. Below in a U. of M. Gopher game, Whitey Skoog, who joined the Lakers after graduation, comes through a tight spot with the ball.

Manufacturing–Blacksmiths
to Electronic Engineers

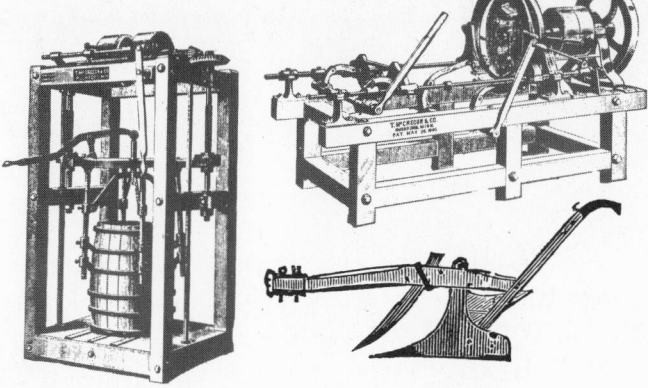

In its early years, Minneapolis, like all frontier villages, depended on the blacksmith shop. And these smithys may be called the beginnings of manufacturing. As sawmills and flour mills came into existence many articles had to be made for them and with the passing of the log cabin era the settlers needed manufactured goods for their new houses.

In 1854 Orrin Rogers, another man from Maine, opened a diminutive sash and door factory. The next year E. Broad began making edged tools. The business was an immediate success and Broad moved into a new shop, stone built, on the east side of Hennepin Island. H. C. Butler began manufacturing tools and mill picks in 1857.

The boom in flour production and the steadily increasing acreage under the plow in Minnesota both fostered Minneapolis manufacturing. Up through the Civil War, local coopers were able to supply barrels for flour but after the war a full scale barrel factory was set up. With the organiza-

tion of the Monitor Plow Works agricultural machinery began to be made in Minneapolis in 1860. The Minneapolis Harvester Works was launched in 1873.

The coming of the railroads also stimulated manufacturing. Northwestern Foundry, established by George Menzel in 1874, turned out car wheels for the early railroad lines.

Viewed from the perspective of today these early manufacturing efforts seem meager. Today Minneapolis employs more than 72,200 workers in strictly manufacturing lines—one-third of the total manufacturing labor force in the entire state of Minnesota. There are 1,500 manufacturing plants in Minneapolis, and Minneapolis manufacturers annually add $535,000,000 to the value of materials processed.

Minneapolis manufacturing divides into three broad general lines: food processing; thermo controls; and metal processing, including the manufacture of machinery. Today Minneapolis products are sold all over

the world. These include agricultural machinery, power mowers and other power equipment, generators, all kinds of thermo controls for home and industry, aviation and atomic instruments, furnaces and heating equipment, motors, processed wood products, mattresses and bedding, underwear, winter and sports clothing, and hundreds of various processed food products.

Some of the outstanding manufacturers in Minneapolis today include General Mills, Minneapolis-Honeywell Regulator Company, Archer-Daniels-Midland Company, Butler Manufacturing Company, B. F. Nelson Manufacturing Co., D. W. Onan & Sons, Minneapolis-Moline, Crown Iron Works, Flour City Ornamental Iron Company, Waterman-Waterbury Company, Salisbury, Munsingwear, Durkee-Atwood, Scott-Atwater, the Gedney Company, Minnesota and Ontario Paper Company, Land O'Lakes, Strutwear, and Toro Manufacturing Company.

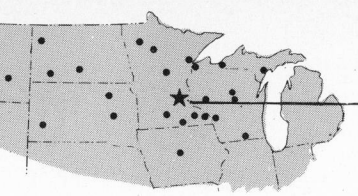

Minneapolis . . . BENSON'S Home Office —
by double choice!

Nearly half a century ago, N. P. Benson — newly arrived from Sweden — *originally* chose Minneapolis as the community in which to set up his small optical workshop. The young N. P. BENSON OPTICAL CO. started out with limited equipment and capital — but with an honest determination to *"make it better."*

During these intervening years, BENSON'S has been happily growing in the sales-fertile Upper Midwest — steadily extending its highly-skilled services to more and more people of this wonderful area.

Today, in addition to our Home Office, there are 27 modern, completely-equipped BENSON branches in strategic locations from Montana to Michigan — and BENSON customers are served by nearly 500 skilled technicians and assistants.

Yes, our Home Office remains here in Minneapolis — *by today's choice!*

One of the spectacles of 1856 — Today glasses are worn by 80% of all Americans compared with 10% one hundred years ago. BENSON'S strict adherence to better design and precision machines operated by highly-skilled technicians have contributed to this industry-wide progress.

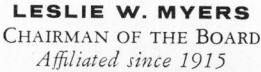

LESLIE W. MYERS
CHAIRMAN OF THE BOARD
Affiliated since 1915

N. P. BENSON
FOUNDER

WILL R. ANDERSON
PRESIDENT
Affiliated since 1914

Benson's

▸ Ground Floor Medical Arts Building
▸ Fourth Floor Medical Arts Building
▸ Also 1610A West Lake Street

In the City of Lakes rogress . . . is for people

Progress is a lot of things in The City of Lakes. It's faith in tomorrow, because someone had faith in yesterday. It's new buildings and fine churches. It's bigger, more productive factories, thriving businesses, new schools that are carrying yesterday's progress into tomorrow. It's all these things and more. Because here progress is for people.

One hundred years ago, those who pioneered this community also could have laid claim to great progress. For then, as now, progress was a way of thinking. And planning. For people.

One hundred years ago—yes, even seventy years ago when Munsingwear first started knitting in this great city—even then progress meant planning ahead. Foreseeing when foresight was difficult. Pioneering when it was safer to stand still.

But it did mean progress. Progress for people.

Progress still means planning ahead, even today. That is why Munsingwear is planning, working, building ahead with the city, the community, the nation it serves. Munsingwear builds for progress. And progress is for people.

People like you find in Minneapolis . . . Minnesota . . . U.S.A.

MUNSINGWEAR NATIONALLY FAMOUS KNIT APPAREL: SLEEPWEAR • UNDERWEAR • SPORTSWEAR

$\mathcal{S}trutwear$ HOSIERY–LINGERIE and BLOUSES

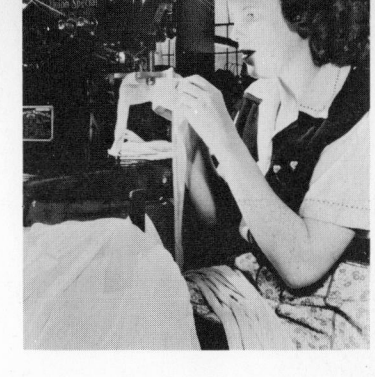

Strutwear views with pride its forty years of growth with Minneapolis, and joins proudly in our city's Centennial Celebration, confident of its future among the people of this great area.

The story of Strutwear is the story of a "hometown" industry that grew steadily in stature and in national recognition. Emphasis upon quality and styling in Strutwear's lines of hosiery, lingerie, and blouses has led to distribution among more than 4500 discriminating retail stores across our nation.

The first Strutwear hosiery was manufactured in Minneapolis in 1916. Continuous expansion resulted in the construction in 1929 of the present home plant with its acres of modern production equipment and its imposing Strutwear tower, a city landmark.

Strutwear success is built upon a foundation of unexcelled employee-management relationship and cooperation. This spirit prevails throughout the company's many branch plants, East, West, and South.

During wartime Strutwear enlisted its plant facilities in our country's cause, and produced 825,000 pairs of uniform pants for our government forces.

Strutwear continuously adds to its experience of the past, by adopting new technological procedures which will better serve our customers everywhere.

$\mathcal{S}trutwear$ MINNEAPOLIS, MINNESOTA

1885

29th Street and Columbus Avenue South, Minneapolis, Minnesota

This is the original factory of Minneapolis-Honeywell. Here the first bimetal home thermostats were produced in 1885. Today, having grown with Minneapolis for almost 75 years, Honeywell is the world's largest manufacturer of automatic controls.

In 9 Minneapolis plants, 14 manufacturing and sales divisions across the country, and 161 world-wide service offices, Honeywell's 25,000 employees produce and sell over 10,000 separate devices. These products control everything from guided missiles to incubators.

More people in Minneapolis share today in Honeywell's progress than any other firm in the Twin Cities.

 **MINNEAPOLIS-HONEYWELL REGULATOR COMPANY**

1877-1956

. . . our 79th year in the pleasant business of manufacturing better, healthier tomorrows.

Imagine . . . a fourth generation of active Minnesotans will be lulled to sleep this very night on a mattress produced by . . .

Salisbury

104 SECOND AVENUE, S.E., MINNEAPOLIS 14.

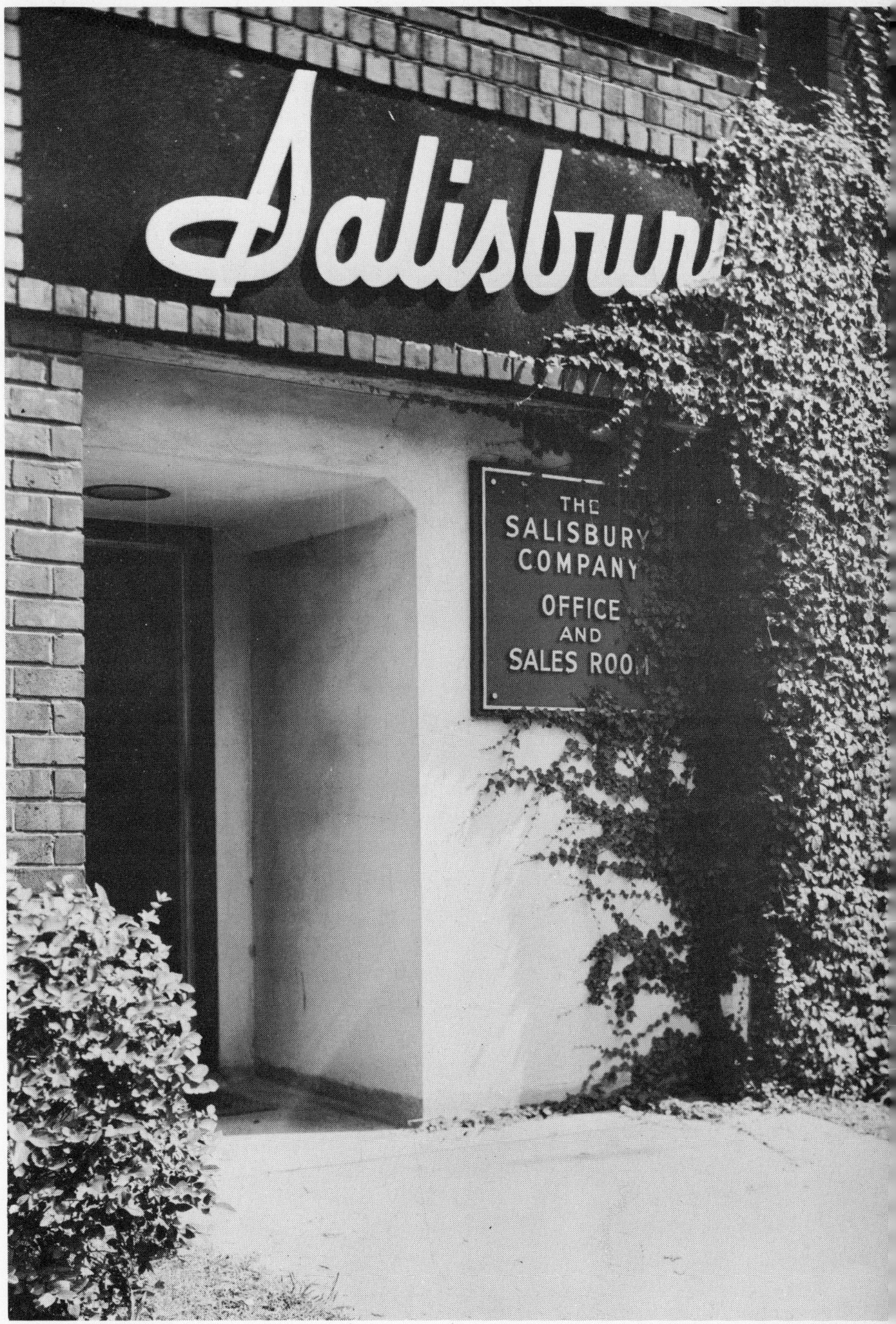

From acetylene lamps and crystal sets to electric lights and "super-hets"

the beginnings of the Onan Company . . . and its progress

BY 1922, all but a few die-hards were convinced that the automobile was here to stay.

Even though manufacturers made claims that their product was perfect, the garage business was booming. To young D. W. Onan, here was an opportunity in the growing motor car industry. In 1922, he began the manufacture of electrical testing equipment for garages, and the product won immediate acceptance.

One of the problems of this business was making boxes for shipping the product. In 1925, to make boxes faster, Onan's developed an engine-driven circular saw. It was so successful in the Onan factory that it was demanded by others. It was named the Safty-Saw and was sold in substantial quantities for use in construction work and in shipping rooms.

In 1926, Onan developed a batteryless D.C. generating plant primarily for summer cottages and small homes beyond the power lines. The electric plant and all the wiring materials were sold as a kit.

A year or two later, the alternating current radio began to replace the battery-operated set. The city dweller could take advantage of this improvement but for the farmer it was a different matter. Neither A.C. radios, nor standard 110-volt A.C. home appliances would work on D.C. current provided by the D.C. generating sets used on farms.

To satisfy this growing need, Onan's developed and built the first small A.C. generating set. It was called the Ten-Lite because it would operate 10 ordinary-size lights at one time. This was enough to light the house and barn, with capacity left over to operate the new super-heterodyne A.C. radio in the living room.

The Onan A.C. generating plant developed a brisk domestic business. And as the reputation of Onan A.C. plants grew, orders began to come in from overseas, stimulated by advertising and the use of Onan plants by missionaries in foreign countries. In many nations of the world, the wonders of electricity were first demonstrated with current from an Onan plant. Even today, in many areas, the name Onan is a synonym for electricity.

In 1934, after years of development, Onan's brought out their own air-cooled engines, built specifically for electric plant use. Connected directly to Onan-built generators, they made possible more compact, sturdier electric plants with length of service far exceeding anything else on the market.

In 1941, the Onan company was the world's foremost producer of electric plants and it was to the Onan company that war procurement agencies turned for military generating sets. At the war's end, Onan had produced more than half of all the electric plants used by our own forces and our allies.

Today Onan produces electric plants of two major types . . .portable electric plants for use where utility power is not available . . . and standby plants for emergency electricity when utility power is interrupted. In addition, Onan air-cooled engines are produced in volume for manufacturers of equipment requiring a premium-grade prime mover.

This is the Age of Electricity . . . and an era of mechanical power . . . creating more uses for both electric plants and engines. Onan has a big stake in these markets today . . . aims at a greater share tomorrow.

 **D. W. ONAN & SONS INC.** • MINNEAPOLIS 14, MINNESOTA

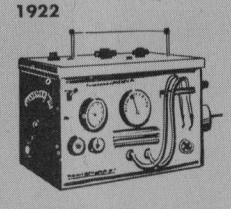

1922

TESTING EQUIPMENT

1925

ONAN SAFTY-SAW

1926

TEN-LITE ELECTRIC PLANT

1934

COMPLETE ONAN PLANTS

1956

AIR-COOLED ENGINES

ELECTRIC PLANTS

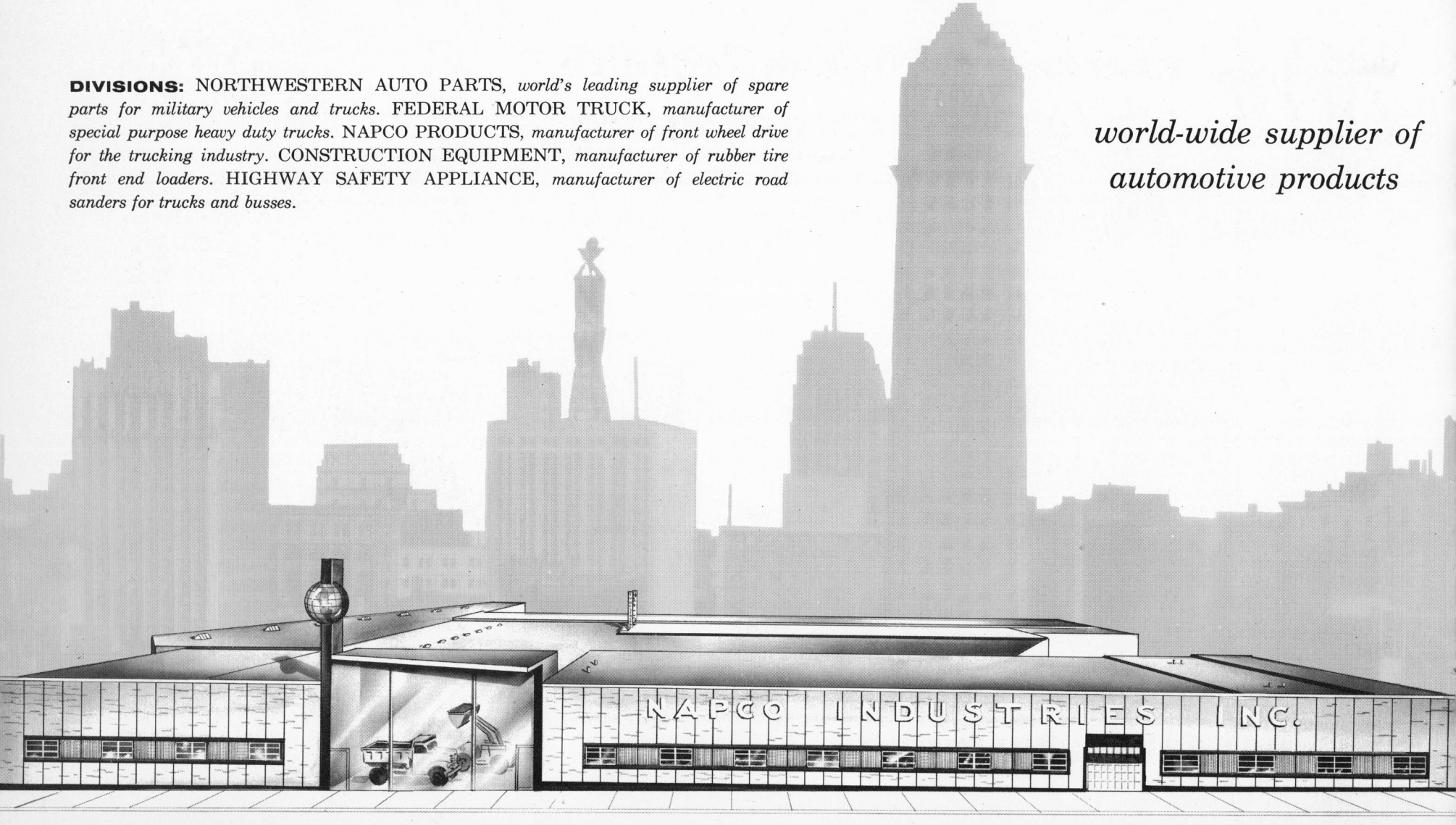

Growing with Minneapolis for 40 years

NAPCO INDUSTRIES, INC.

DIVISIONS: NORTHWESTERN AUTO PARTS, *world's leading supplier of spare parts for military vehicles and trucks.* FEDERAL MOTOR TRUCK, *manufacturer of special purpose heavy duty trucks.* NAPCO PRODUCTS, *manufacturer of front wheel drive for the trucking industry.* CONSTRUCTION EQUIPMENT, *manufacturer of rubber tire front end loaders.* HIGHWAY SAFETY APPLIANCE, *manufacturer of electric road sanders for trucks and busses.*

world-wide supplier of automotive products

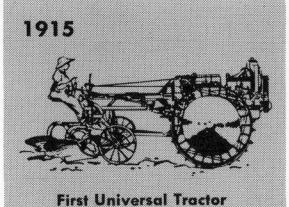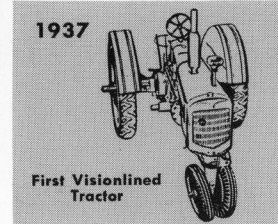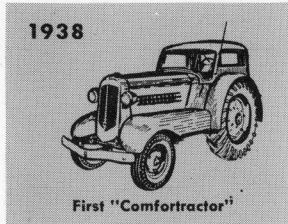

FROM 1893 TO 1956
FLOUR CITY PROGRESS
SIXTY-THREE YEARS OF CONSISTENT GROWTH IN MINNEAPOLIS

In 1893, Eugene Tetzlaff, a man endowed with skill, vision and determination, leased a former stable on Fourth Avenue South and erected a sign fashioned by his own hands which announced the opening of the Flour City Ornamental Iron Company.

This was the era during which our country was emerging from the pioneer phase of American history. Already the structural steel frame for building construction had been tried and proven . . . heralding the birth of our modern skyscraper.

Eugene Tetzlaff sensed the opportunities opened by new construction methods and techniques, and his enthusiasm was reflected in his early partners—Ernest Rubbert, Fred Schilling and Louis Volmer. With Eugene at the forge, Ernest and Fred fitting and assembling, and Louis keeping books, Flour City began its growth. Sixty-three years later, Flour City has emerged one of Minneapolis' major businesses, with main plant facilities occupying a complete square block, plus large additional facilities for the production and warehousing of Aluma Craft boats. Business of today has come a long way from the early days of "Everything in wire, wrought iron and brass work, any finish. Designs and estimates cheerfully furnished". Today's estimates, still cheerfully furnished, include many for complete metal "skins" such as that for the Lutheran Brotherhood Building pictured left. Here Flour City fabricated stainless steel frames, with insulated panels of porcelain-enameled steel, to form a light, efficient curtain wall for this modern structure.

No longer hand-forged, today's panels and windows are pressed on giant hydraulic presses or extruded into desired sections.

Today Flour City operates on an international scope, with no task too large.

Flour City is proud of its progress . . . as it is proud of the city in which this growth was possible, and it is with sixty-three years of enthusiasm that Flour City congratulates Minneapolis in this centennial year.

ARCHITECTS:
Perkins & Will, Chicago, Illinois

GENERAL CONTRACTOR:
Kraus-Anderson, Inc.
Minneapolis, Minnesota

The FLOUR CITY Ornamental IRON COMPANY
2637 27TH AVENUE SOUTH • MINNEAPOLIS, MINNESOTA

It's the revolutionary new

TORO
"POWER HANDLE"

by

TORO MANUFACTURING CORP.

3030 Snelling Avenue • Minneapolis 6

Makers of home power tools and the world's most complete line of power mowing equipment

A MECHANICAL HANDYMAN you'll use in all four seasons! The Toro "Power Handle" is a demountable 2¾ hp gasoline engine that switches in seconds from one Toro work unit to another. Work units now include (counter-clockwise): 17-inch Snow Hound rotary snow plow, 110-volt generator, tiller, 20-inch self-propelled Whirlwind rotary mower, 21-inch self-propelled Sportlawn reel mower, edger-trimmer, power pump, power sprayer. And new work units are on the way! See the "Power Handle" at your Toro dealer's — his name is in your classified phone book under "Lawn Mowers".

Now—FLOOR CARE CAN BE
Child's Play!

Here's the truly easy way to keep your floors safe, looking bright and sparkling clean. You can actually scrub, wax, or polish your floors so effortless you'll hardly know you're doing it.

The ADVANCE "Gyro-12" is the ideal floor machine for the home or moderate size office or store.

With its greater weight per square inch of brush area, the perfectly balanced "Gyro-12" gives professional results—yet can be operated by anyone—even a child.

Find out how economically you can have the time-saving, work-saving "Gyro-12" floor machine in your own office, store, or home. Call or write ADVANCE MACHINE COMPANY, 4100 Washington Avenue North, Minneapolis, for a free test demonstration.

Call or write for a free demonstration in your own office, store, or home.

Four Generations in ADVANCE MACHINES

Six-year-old Polly Pond, shown operating floor machine, is the first member of the fourth generation of the Pond family to sell equipment made by ADVANCE MACHINE COMPANY.

MERRIT G. POND
Founder - 1910

HAROLD J. POND
President

ROBERT J. POND
Vice President

Manufacturers of a complete line of floor and rug maintenance machines, and Terrazzo surfacing equipment.

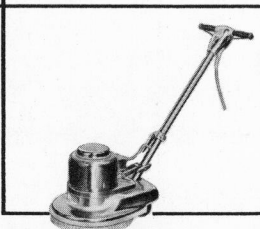

ADVANCE "Hydro-Jet" Industrial Vacs.

All new square design and other exclusive features make the "Hydro-Jet" the most efficient, easiest to operate wet or dry vacuum on the market today.

ADVANCE Terrazzo Surfacing Machines

Over 80% of all Terrazzo floors installed in this country are ground with ADVANCE Machines.

ADVANCE Rug and Floor Maintenance Machines

A machine for every industrial or household need. Scrubbing - Polishing - Steelwooling - Waxing - Sanding.

Gyro 12
®

ADVANCE
®

ADVANCE MACHINE COMPANY
4100 WASHINGTON AVENUE NORTH
MINNEAPOLIS, MINN.

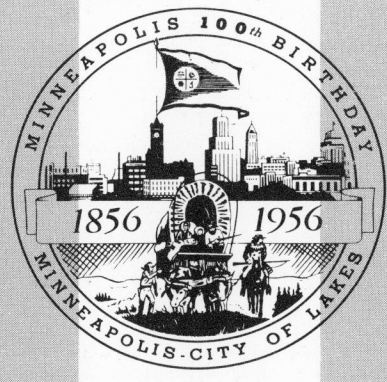

TOO BIG?

Minneapolis is not too big—as cities go. Not too big, for example, to have a neighborly pride in schools, hospitals and parks. Not too big to have people who are easy to meet, easy to live with. For our part, as a company that has grown up here during the last 49 years, we've always felt that *people* are the promise of Minneapolis. Because of them, our community—on its 100th birthday—is undergoing the greatest business and industrial expansion in its history!

The **Waterman-Waterbury** Company **Waterburg** MANUFACTURERS OF WORLD-FAMOUS FURNACES AND AIR CONDITIONERS

HOME OFFICE AND FACTORY: MINNEAPOLIS, MINNESOTA

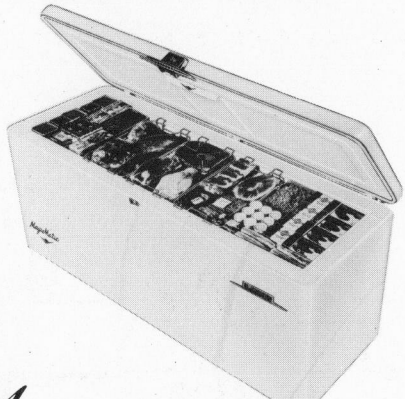

AQUATENNIAL—

City of Lakes' Summer Playtime

The Minneapolis Aquatennial probably would have developed anyway — it was a natural — but a visit of the King and Queen of England to Winnipeg in 1939 speeded up events.

King George VI and Queen Elizabeth (now the Queen Mother) were making a tour of Canada and a group of Minneapolis men, as a neighborly gesture, were delegated to go to Winnipeg and take part in Manitoba's royal welcome and celebration. It was just the right psychological moment.

In the Nineteen Thirties, Minneapolis had suffered some adverse national publicity. It had been tagged as a city of strikes and gang killings. We had been visited by Dillinger and the Karpis and Barker mobs. Many Minneapolitans were restive and nervous when visitors said, "Take us some place where we can see some gangsters."

As 1939 drew on many people were turning over ideas for improving the city's national public relations. Some thought we should make better use of the lakes and

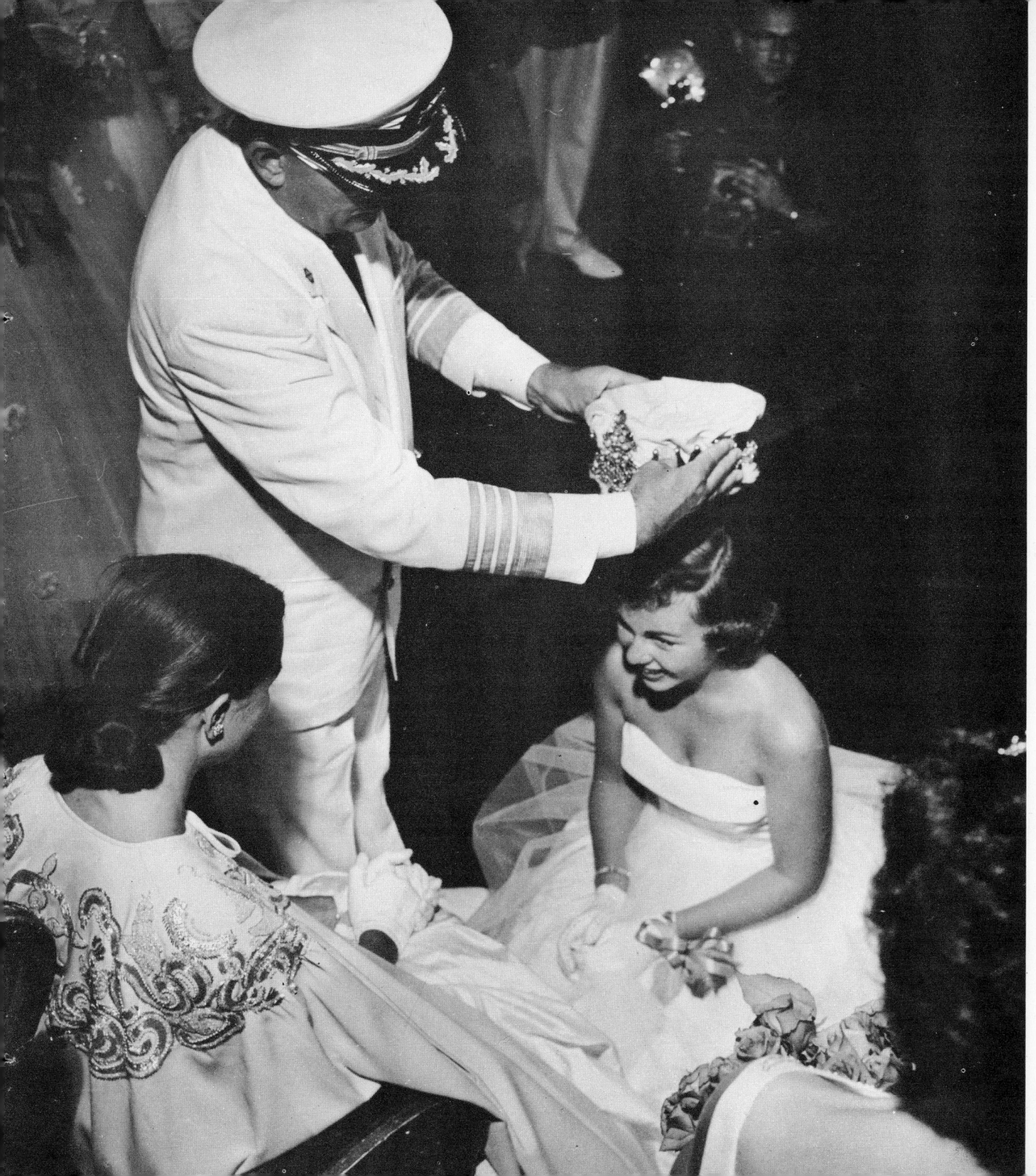

All Aquatennial is poised here. The blur of 120 Aquatennial events comes into a sharp, fine focus . . . a climactic crescendo when the glittering crown of the Queen of the Lakes is lifted and placed on the head of the new Queen at Aquatennial Star Night and Coronation, sponsored by the Minneapolis Star and Tribune. For ten days 40 candidates from throughout Minnesota are sparkle-eyed . . . a sense of urgency mounts as the coronation moment draws near . . . hair is smoothed, gowns straightened . . . 18,000 people in the Parade Stadium are hushed . . . The Aquatennial Commodore walks slowly down a frothy line of 40 breathless beauties. Then it's over with a roar of the crowd and a blaze of fireworks. The new Queen of the Lakes, titular ruler of our summer season has been chosen. The Aquatennial president places the crown on her head, and Minneapolis has a Queen . . . symbol of all we treasure in our city . . . and of what we have to say to the nation.

parks as vacation and playtime resources. Others thought that many more visitors could be attracted to the city — if only we had something . . . But what was it to be?

It was at this point that a Chamber of Commerce group headed north for Winnipeg. The day of the royal arrival was rainy. Undaunted, loyal Canadians turned out by the tens of thousands to see their King and Queen. Sitting soaked in the bleachers on a rain-swept Winnipeg street were Dave Onan, then convention chairman of the Minneapolis Civic and Commerce Association (as it was called at that time); Tom Hastings and Publicity Man Mike Fadell.

"If we only had this crowd in Minneapolis and it wasn't raining," Fadell remarked.

"We could get a lot more people if we had a natural attraction like this," Onan observed.

"Why not put on a big show?" Hastings asked, "like the St. Paul winter carnival — only in the summertime."

And right there, Aquatennial was on its way.

Back in Minneapolis it was necessary to have meetings and organize committees. Minneapolis Sports and Attractions, Inc., was formed. Alfred D. Lindley, mountain climber and later state legislator, a lawyer, drew up the incorporation papers. Hastings was elected president; Henry Baker, vice president; Pat Carr, secretary, and Dick Kitchen, treasurer. An executive committee was formed which included, besides the of-

136

ficers, George Adams, John C. Cornelius, Earl Gammons, L. J. Ludwig, Neil R. Messick, E. T. Palmer, Walter Quist, Arthur Randall, W. R. Stephens, Al Swanson and Lindley. Stephens was named chairman for the 1940 celebration.

A name was needed for the big summer festival and a contest was held for suggestions. The winner was Rudolph Willer, at that time a young bridegroom. His idea brought him $50. The name was coined out of two Greek words, aqua, meaning water, and tennial, meaning annual.

Today more than 1,000 Minneapolis business men and civic leaders form the core for the annual festival. They operate on the theory that a city, like a business, has to be promoted — or the customers go elsewhere. The Aquatennial management believes in and is concerned with the growth of Minneapolis — culturally, economically and recreationally.

"Of the 1,653,000 persons vacationing at Minnesota resorts and camps in 1953," a statement of the Aquatennial Association points out, "more than 50 per cent of a sample polled by Minnesota Poll interviewers listed Aquatennial as one of the reasons for their coming to the state . . . Aqua officials have no illusions about Aquatennial being the sole reason for attracting all these tourists. They do maintain that Aquatennial is one of the important factors in pulling tourists in a state where this business is number three in gross income. During the festival in Minneapolis over 1,000,000 persons take part in one or more events . . . Conservative estimates reveal that over 100,-000 out of staters visit Minneapolis solely for Aquatennial."

From a participation standpoint, the giant summer festival brings together almost every element in the city. About 7,000 persons take part in the two big parades. More than 25,000 are in the music sections of the show. Another 50,000 are in the sports program. Five hundred beautiful girls compete for Queen of the Lakes. Swimming brings out 200 AAU swimmers and 119 swimming and diving stars are in the Aqua Follies, with a total cast of nearly 2,000 in the big lake show.

Focal points in the ten-day festival are the two giant parades — the day parade and the dazzling torchlight parade. Bands, floats and marching units from every corner of the nation wind their way down Minneapolis' fashion boulevard, Nicollet Avenue.

Crowning event in the Aquatennial is the selection of the Queen of the Lakes, the titular ruler of the Minneapolis summer season. Forty carefully selected girls, representing organizations and communities throughout Minnesota, are in the finals for this honor. They are examined and re-examined during the ten-day event on the basis of wholesome personality and beauty. The climax comes when the new Queen of the Lakes is crowned in a glittering coronation ceremony usually held under the stars at the Minneapolis Parade stadium.

Meaning is given to the tired words, "The Greatest Show on Earth" by Aqua Follies, a water spectacle born, reared, that has reached full growth in Minneapolis. Graceful water ballet, Olympic diving, precision swimming, comic diving . . . staged at the Aqua Follies pool overlooking emerald-hued Theodore Wirth lake . . . make the event a part of the heritage of our city.

The picturesque pool provides an inspirational setting for the Interdenominational Religious Services at which the white-clad Naval Aviation Cadet choir from Pensacola, Fla. traditionally sings as part of the military participation by all armed forces branches in Aquatennial.

Living, playing, working near the water in Minneapolis is the theme of existence, the elixir of life . . . Aquatennial communicates this for Minneapolitans to the nation.

Each day has a special "tag" during the Aquatennial. Legislators, editors, mayors, and children all receive their share of the limelight. Most inspirational event of the entire festival is the interdenominational religious service. It has become traditional that the Naval cadet choir from Pensacola, Fla., sings a program of sacred music and visiting religious leaders deliver sermons.

The Aqua sports program reads like an encyclopedia of summer athletics. The list includes regattas, swimming and diving, fly and bait casting, power boat races, track and field events, tennis, golf, shuffleboard, horseshoes, badminton and other events.

The objectives of this great Upper Midwest summer show are stated in the by-laws of the association. These are:

"To advance and promote the civic betterment and general welfare of the City of Minneapolis, its trade and commerce and its religious and educational life, by providing recreation and entertainment for all classes and persons and by improving the physical and moral and mental condition of its people;

"To advance the commercial, economic, social, musical and athletic interest within the municipality;

"To create a spirit of goodwill and friendliness among the people of this community and those living elsewhere in the state and union;

"To provide a program of sports and attractions for the common interest of the people in the community and,

"To promote, produce and stage such events and attractions as shall appeal to the citizens of Minneapolis and shall attract guests and visitors."

140

Festival fills the air at Aquatennial time. The watch-charm counterparts of the Queen of the Lakes and Commodore are chosen . . . Aqua Jesters, anonymous businessmen's clown club, weave a thread of comedy throughout the festival . . . color-splashed pageantry of parades and parties—coronation and concerts . . . 120 events—of which 115 are free to the public . . . all spell Aquatennial, when enthusiasm about Minneapolis bubbles to the surface and we tell the world through the Aquatennial festival. In a class by itself is the WCCO-Aquatennial Radio Show. Magic names of celebrities . . . Bob Hope, Ken Murray, Arthur Godfrey, the McGuire Sisters, Peter Lind Hayes, and Mary Healy . . . take part in a locally aired radio show that thrills Minneapolis. The celebrities love our city of lakes . . . and they add lustre to the Minneapolis Centennial, climaxed this year by the Aquatennial.

A parade float created early in our city's history during the 19th century proclaimed, "Let us make our whole city beautiful." It was then the spirit of Aquatennial was born. The dimension of communication . . . telling people of our beautiful city . . . was added when the "Aquatennial Idea" took shape in 1939. Parades . . . not just a parade, but the best . . . was a vehicle through which the Aquatennial story evolved. There are 120 other events that are other ways Aquatennial tells the Minneapolis story.

With parades came decorations and Minneapolis' fashion boulevard, Nicollet avenue, was made festive by the first Aquatennial street decorations in 1940.

The avenue of approach to the Parade Ground for the Grand Aquatennial Day Parade and the Torchlight Parade was punctuated by flags and recreational statues with a huge archway through which the first Aquatennial parade marched in 1940.

And when the Aquatennial pioneers of 1940 were finished . . . the parade at the right is what they had.

The Queen of the Lakes is crowned. It's as exciting now as in 1940. The new Queen of the Lakes to be named this year at Aquatennial Star Night and Coronation will symbolize more . . . she will crystallize the climax of Minneapolis Centennial.

Visitations to civic clubs, cities and celebrations throughout Minneapolis, the state and the nation was one way of telling the Minneapolis story conceived by the pioneers in 1940. The first visitation was made to the Mayor of Minneapolis. Since then, Aquatennial has averaged over 100 visitations throughout a year from coast to coast and to Europe.

The first of Aquatennial's board of directors believed in Minneapolis. They worked hard. They begot Aquatennial, first a dream in 1939 before a reality in 1940, and their policies are being followed today, when the Minneapolis Centennial climax will be embodied in Aquatennial.

The Queen of the Lakes event grew out of those fertile minds as a way of symbolizing the Minneapolis way of life and telling the nation about it. The first Queen of the Lakes judging was held at the Nicollet hotel.

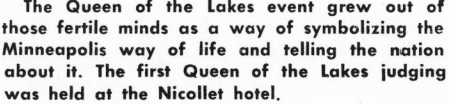

James M. Goodhue

FAVORITE

GRAPHIC ARTS —
Vital Communications Link

James Madison Goodhue, who had published the Grant County Herald at Lancaster, Wisconsin, arrived in the new territory of Minnesota in 1849, bringing with him the first printing press. His "Minnesota Pioneer," published in St. Paul was the first printing produced in the Minnesota country.

Shortly after that, a missionary carried a printing press into what was then the wilderness around Cass Lake. In 1851, Elmer Tyler, a tailor, and Isaac Atwater, a lawyer, printed the first edition of the "St. Anthony Express"—and printing came into its own in Minneapolis.

Job printing followed the establishment of newspapers. There were small lots of handbills to be printed for local merchants. As the city grew, there were tickets to be run off for special events. Business men wanted all kinds of printed articles—stationery, envelopes, bills, mailing tags, account sheets and cards for birthdays and holidays.

"The job printer was called upon to do more and more tasks," says an historical statement from the Graphic Arts Industries of Minneapolis. "He had to put in new equipment that would handle his new demands. He had to have paper, type machinery, ink and illustrations."

Today, there are in Minneapolis more than 400 firms engaged, in one way or another, in the Graphic Arts Industries. These firms, at the latest count, employ 8,285 persons and have an annual payroll of almost $36,000,000 a year.

"Not only is printing, the art preservative, one of the greatest of all arts," continues the statement of the Graphic Arts Industries, "but taking in those industries whose chief function is to supply its materials, it is the greatest of all American industries. Even excluding the paper industry, the greater part of whose annual billion dollar a year product is used to carry the printed word; the printing machinery industry, the printing ink industry; and other industries directly connected with it, the printing, publishing and allied industries, according to the United States census figures, rank first in number of establishments; first in value added by manufacture; first in number of salaried employees; first in salaries paid; third in wages paid; fifth in number of wage earners, and fifth in value of products."

MINNEAPOLIS, *we Salute you!*

We salute you and the people and industries that have made possible your growth and prosperity.

We are happy to be located in this progressive city and proud to be representing the Paper Industry which has contributed so much to the advancement of our standard of living in Minneapolis and the entire nation.

1956

1856

In 1856 the annual per capita paper consumption was 4.5 pounds.
In 1956 the per capita consumption is estimated at 420 pounds.

MINNESOTA PAPER AND CORDAGE COMPANY

DISTRIBUTORS OF PRINTING PAPERS, INDUSTRIAL PAPERS AND PACKAGING PAPERS TO THE UPPER MIDWEST

Since 1871

We at Harrison and Smith are proud of our association for many, many years with companies who have contributed so much to the growth of Minneapolis. We are pleased that we have been able to keep pace with their ever-increasing demand for finer printed material.

HARRISON and SMITH

520 Washington Avenue No.
Minneapolis 1, Minnesota

Congratulations

Minneapolis – Our City – on your 100th Birthday

1856   1956   2056

It has been our privilege and good fortune for the past 74 years to have grown and succeeded with you. We are anticipating with pleasure our joint growth and success in the next 100 years.

1882   1956   2056

McGill Company

PRINTERS AND LITHOGRAPHERS

501 PARK AVENUE • MINNEAPOLIS 15, MINNESOTA

DESIGN ★ COPY ★ LAYOUT ★ ENGRAVING ★ CREATIVE IDEAS ★ TYPESETTING

The Colwell Press

63 YEARS
OF FINE PRINTING

The House of Craftsmen

It was in 1893 that T. H. Colwell set up a small printing shop practically under the railroad bridge at Fourteenth Avenue. Known as the "University printer," Mr. Colwell built up a solid reputation for integrity and fine craftsmanship — a reputation that has endured.

From such a modest beginning, The Colwell Press soon outgrew its quarters on the University campus and made the first of what was to be a series of moves. And as the little company progressed, it several times merged with other printing firms, consolidating them under the Colwell escutcheon.

In 1927, The Colwell Press moved into the Daily News Building (now the Treasure Masters Building), where the company flourished for 21 years. By 1948, the firm again was beset with "growing pains," necessitating another move. This time, The Colwell Press didn't abandon its quarters entirely, but retained the second floor. The bulk of the printing equipment and the general offices were moved to our present location at 501-13 South Sixth Street.

The policy of the leadership of The Colwell Press remains today the same as it was in 1893 — to produce top quality printing and to take an active part in civic, church and industrial affairs, both locally and nationally.

Along the way, through the years, we at The Colwell Press have made many friends in these pursuits. Naturally, we are proud of our growth and progress in the graphic arts industry, but we must acknowledge that our development is a result of the faith and confidence that the many fine business and industrial firms have placed in us.

As we celebrate this Centennial year, we wish to salute the hundreds of Minnesota firms who have "grown up" with us and before us. We take pride in the knowledge that so many of them have made it a habit to call on The Colwell Press whenever they wish to order fine printing.

1856 MINNEAPOLIS 1956

*It is a pleasure to look back over 30 of
those years in business in a progressive city.*

Congratulations Minneapolis!

Printing Inc.

4325 HIAWATHA AVENUE • **PArkway 2-6655**

LETTERPRESS

LITHOGRAPHY

COMPOSITION

BINDERY

an historic parallel

1856
*First Bridge Across the
Mississippi River*

1905
First Jensen Plant

1955
New Jensen Plant

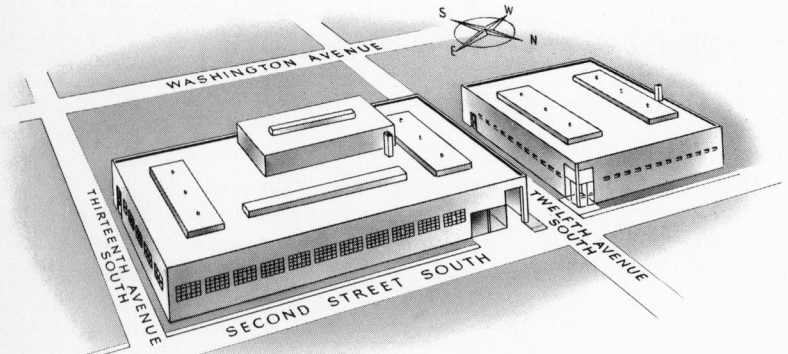

In one hundred years Minneapolis has grown, flourished and developed into one of the major cities in our nation. We are indebted to our ancestry and proud of our surrounding legend steeped in Bunyanesque feats and Indian lore.

Likewise, in one-half century, Jensen Printing has earned its leadership in Graphic Arts in the Upper Midwest.

Just as Minneapolis will continue to expand according to the needs of our country, so will Jensen keep pace with the needs and demands of Midwest businesses.

So, with pride and gratitude, Jensen Printing Company congratulates Minneapolis during this Centennial Celebration. Her success has directly affected our own.

JENSEN PRINTING COMPANY
200 Twelfth Avenue South
Minneapolis 15, Minn.

ONE HUNDRED YEARS OF PROGRESS — FIFTY YEARS OF PRINTING

Our Story of Progress...
years of growing with Minneapolis!

Two years before the turn of the century, a young easterner was working as an artist on a San Francisco newspaper. This, in itself, was nothing unusual. One thing was unusual, however—he had traveled all the way from Buffalo to the Golden Gate under his own power, *by bicycle!*

The youthful artist was Edwin F. Bauer, a man whose dynamic personality was soon to make itself felt in the business life of the Midwest's fast-growing

lumber and milling city . . . Minneapolis. He was happy in the West, but a chance to go back home by rail at a reduced rate proved too attractive to pass up. The railroad's route was through Minneapolis. More or less on a hunch, Bauer decided to stop off and see the sights.

The thriving town looked good to him and, then and there, he resolved to cast his lot with the fortunes of the community and its citizens!

It was the Fall of 1898. James Gray was Mayor and the great new Court House and City Hall was in its ninth year of building. The Public Library, Donaldson's Glass Block, Grain Exchange, New York Life building, First Baptist church and many other fine edifices dotted the downtown area. Here was a ripe location for an art studio and Edwin Bauer lost no time hanging out "his shingle" in the old Globe building on Nicollet avenue. The little studio, dubbed "Bureau of Design," did well from the start.

By 1908, a considerable metamorphosis had taken place in the new art studio. It had expanded its services into the photoengraving field and was now known as the Bureau of Engraving. Mr. Bauer had been joined

by Robert M. Schmerler and John C. Buckbee, father of the Bureau's present head. Larger quarters in the brand new Warner Hardware building at 15 South Sixth Street became the firm's fourth location in its 10-year history.

Progress with Minneapolis was the rule, and in 1914 the Bureau's officers, along with J. J. Sher, E. S. Smith, Joseph Almars and Colgate Buckbee launched an amazing new venture that was destined to make art

Draw Me!

history. Commercial artists were scarce. Industries the nation over demanded more and more of them to illustrate advertising matter. So, these men of the Bureau founded Federal Schools (later named Art Instruction, Inc.) which set out to offer home study training in commercial art, illustrating and cartooning. The pretty "Draw Me Girl" featured in the school's advertising was soon familiar to people in every state in the Union and in many foreign countries as well. Today, Art Instruction, Inc., is the world's largest home study art school and is a wholly owned subsidiary of the Bureau.

An important program of expansion was instituted in 1920 when the organization moved to its present building at 500 South Fourth Street. As early as 1908, a small printing department had been established, but now a full scale Letterpress Division, Composing Room and Bindery went into operation. Four years later, "Growing With Minneapolis" had become such a habit that the firm was again bursting at the seams

and a handsome new "school building" was erected to provide the finest home study art school quarters in the country.

To keep pace with the fast-moving trends in the graphic arts field, the Bureau added an offset lithography division in 1932. The forward move greatly enhanced the firm's competitive position. This, in turn, set up a chain reaction which resulted in a steady increase in facilities throughout the depression and World War II years.

The Bureau's splendid "all under one roof" graphic arts services have indeed continued to grow with Minneapolis. Clear evidence of this fact is its roster of customers . . . business and industrial firms that are known from coast to coast. And as milling and lumbering flourished back in 1898, famous flour mills and lumber products companies still are vital local industries—and customers of the Bureau!

Yes, today, 1956, the Bureau of Engraving, Inc., continues to demonstrate unique ability to apply its craftsmanship and experience in new fields. A recently organized Industrial Division now offers an extensive variety of etched wiring circuits to the mushrooming electronics industry.

We salute Minneapolis in its glorious Centennial Year. We are indeed proud that for fifty-eight active years we have grown with the great city that saw its beginnings by the Falls of St. Anthony!

BUREAU OF ENGRAVING, INC. • ART INSTRUCTION, INC.
500 South Fourth Street, Minneapolis 15, Minnesota

Isaac Atwater

Minneapolis Newspapers

On May 31, 1851, the St. Anthony Express, the community's first newspaper, made its appearance. It was printed in the old log mess house used by the men who built the first sawmill on the east side. Judge Isaac Atwater was the editor.

Years later the Judge, in a reminiscent mood, remarked: "The subscribers agreed to pay two dollars a year, and really intended to do so. But, alas, the human necessity of daily bread was often greater than the necessity of a weekly newspaper. Hence they were forced to compromise on the amount of their subscriptions in farm produce, boots, clothing and groceries, and not seldom, promises only."

A year after the paper's first publication it was taken over by George D. Bowman, a newspaperman from Pennsylvania. Three years later, in 1855, Judge Atwater, who had made cash advances to the paper for which he was writing editorials, took possession to protect his investment.

The second newspaper, the Northwestern Democrat, appeared in the summer of 1853. In 1854 this was moved across the river and the name was changed to the Minneapolis Democrat. It was the first newspaper published west of the Mississippi and north of Iowa.

In the following years newspapers blossomed like wildflowers. In 1858, a weekly called the Minneapolis Journal was launched. It merged a short time later with the State Atlas. The St. Anthony Republican, the Cataract and Agriculturalist, the Independent, the Minneapolis Plaindealer, the Rural Minnesotan, the Minnesota Beacon — these were some of the pioneer newspapers.

In May, 1859, Colonel William S. King, a native New Yorker who had known Thurlow Weed and William H. Seward in the organization days of the Republican party in New York, started the State Atlas. This was merged a few years later with the

Weekly Chronicle. It made its first appearance under a new name on May 25, 1867. The name was the Minneapolis Tribune.

November 26, 1878, the Evening Journal appeared. In 1885 the Journal was sold to A. J. Blethen, W. E. Haskell, H. W. Hawley, and Lucian Swift for $130,000. In 1905 a Sunday morning edition of the Journal appeared. And in 1908 the paper was acquired by Herschel V. and William S. Jones.

The Star, a six-day evening paper, was established in 1920, and from 1924 to 1935 it was published by John Thompson, former executive of the New York Times. In 1935, John and Gardner Cowles, who had been active in the management of the Des Moines Register and Tribune, purchased the Star.

Shortly after the sale John Cowles moved to Minneapolis with his family and purchased a home here. New editing tech-

It takes 14,000 of your neighbors to create, produce and distribute the Minneapolis Star and Minneapolis Tribune

● A well-informed people is the necessary foundation for progress in a community, in an area, in a nation. Serving this vital need for news and information is the proud task to which 14,000 of your friends and neighbors are dedicated. The more than 2,000 men and women at the Minneapolis Star and Tribune plant, and the 12,000 Star and Tribune carriers and farm route men throughout the Upper Midwest, are bringing the world to your doorstep each day through the pages of the Minneapolis Star and the Minneapolis Tribune.

Only the 4 largest cities in the United States have newspapers with more circulation than the Minneapolis Sunday Tribune

SINCE 1883, A. J. DAHL COMPANY HAS BEEN THE NORTHWEST'S LEADING BOOKBINDERS

The first books were delivered by push cart to a carriage barn out on Minnehaha Avenue. This was the first home of the A. J. Dahl Company. Today, huge semi-truck trailers deliver and pick up thousands of books from a large three story building on Chicago Avenue. This building now houses the present company and the newly purchased Oliver Baker Manufacturing Company, manufacturers of loose-leaf binders, leather and advertising specialties since 1900.

Congratulations, Minneapolis, on your Centennial. Thanks to you, readers of books, and the printers and publishers for helping the Graphic Arts industry and its employees to grow with you.

A. J. DAHL COMPANY
416 CHICAGO AVENUE • MINNEAPOLIS

A number of years ago books were sewn by hand on a sewing rack. Today they are sewn on a battery of high-speed automatic machines.

A family affair

CARL J. MJOS,
and five sons own
and operate the company.

C. J. MJOS
President
General Manager

CLARENCE B. MJOS
Vice-President
Production
Maintenance

O. L. (BUD) MJOS
Treasurer
Purchasing
Estimating
Sales

JOHN G. MJOS
Forwarding
Department

EDWARD N. MJOS
Secretary
Production
Manager

CARL J. MJOS, JR.
Casemaking
Department

✶ *The Most Modern Equipped Edition Bindery in the Northwest*

niques and methods were adopted which soon caused the Star to be discussed by newspaper people throughout the nation. By 1939, the Star's circulation had doubled and the Star was the largest and leading daily newspaper in Minneapolis.

August 1, 1939, the Minneapolis Star purchased the Journal. The two evening papers were combined as the Star Journal. Under new ownership the Sunday Star Journal began to grow rapidly. A new building was started in the fall of 1939 and was completed and dedicated in the summer of 1940.

There was a re-alignment of all Minneapolis newspapers May 1, 1941. The depression of the thirties had made inroads on newspapers along with other businesses, and all Minneapolis papers were faced with tremendous increased costs. The re-alignment was essential if Minneapolis was to have really outstanding newspapers. The Sunday Star Journal was combined with and called the Sunday Tribune.

The Sunday Tribune now has circulation in excess of 625,000 copies. The combined circulation of the Star and Morning Tribune totals more than 495,000. Only four cities in the United States — New York, Chicago, Philadelphia, and Los Angeles—have newspapers with larger circulations than the Minneapolis Sunday Tribune.

The Minneapolis Star and Tribune are published in one of the finest newspaper plants in the world. Dedicated in 1949, the building spans an entire city block on Portland Avenue between Fourth and Fifth Streets.

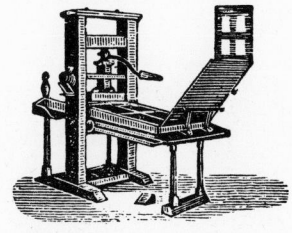

THE LOCAL 1145 AFL—HONEYWELL STORY

Minnesota's largest Union . . . Local 1145 AFL and Minnesota's largest company . . . Honeywell, through excellent labor relations, are helping to build a greater Minneapolis.

"Team" means more jobs for Minneapolis, means millions of dollars in purchasing power to our community. We are proud of Minneapolis . . . we are proud of our labor relations between Local 1145 AFL and Minneapolis Honeywell.

"TEAM" ...MEANS PROGRESS FOR MINNEAPOLIS

A SUCCESS STORY IN LABOR RELATIONS BETWEEN LOCAL 1145 AFL AND HONEYWELL

Across the table bargaining has brought uninterrupted production for 15 years. Beneficiaries: Our community, our State, our Nation.

LOCAL 1145, AT HONEYWELL

MINNEAPOLIS PROGRESS IS BUILT ON

Manpower

The manpower of Minneapolis has continually forged ahead and has made Minneapolis a better place to live since way back when a charter was issued on December 11, 1903, for the formation of a city central federation of A.F. of L. local unions by the American Federation of Labor for the city of Minneapolis.

From a handful of local unions representing a few hundred members, that federation has grown and kept pace with the growth and progress of our community until today we represent 173 affiliated local unions comprising over 85,000 members, who with their families comprise nearly one-fourth of a million people — almost half of the population of our great city.

We are proud to be a part of every worthwhile civic activity which denotes progress for our city and its people.

CENTRAL LABOR UNION OF MINNEAPOLIS

Hotels—The Story of Public Hospitality

Schiek's in 1904 was one of the famous restaurants of Minneapolis and its reputation as a good eating place continues to the present time.

The Nicollet House was built in 1857 at the corner of Washington and Hennepin Avenues and opened for business on May 20, 1858, and immediately established a reputation with the traveling public. The present Nicollet Hotel was built on the same location.

In pioneer times there was a little slab-built house down near St. Anthony Falls. The village called it "The Strangers' House." New arrivals were welcome to stay here until they could build a place of their own. They were also welcome to eat at the Mess House, built for the men working on the first mill. These were the first "hotel" accommodations in the new village.

As the river settlements grew in the 1850's, boarding and rooming houses sprang up on both east and west sides. By the middle 1850's there was an increasing demand for a good hotel. In 1856, J. M. Winslow launched plans for a six-story stone-built hotel overlooking the falls. It was opened in the spring of 1857.

The Winslow House immediately became popular with southern visitors. In those years, preceding the Civil War, wealthy southerners came north in the summer, and Minnesota, then as now, was considered the choicest of vacation spots. The coming of the war ruined the Winslow House trade. It remained unoccupied until 1872 and was then used for a few years by Macalester College and the Minnesota College Hospital. In 1887 it was torn down to make way for the old Exposition building.

Meanwhile, across the river on the west side, plans were being pushed for a first-class hotel. This was the old Nicollet House at Washington and Hennepin Avenues. Henry T. Welles, former mayor of St. Anthony, and others raised $10,000 for the hotel by private subscription. It was opened May 20, 1858, an imposing six-story structure of cream brick. For many years it was a center of social life in the city.

By the 1880's, the growing city was again feeling the need for a new, first-class hotel. John T. West, a young restaurant man, had taken over the Nicollet House. West was visited by his uncle, Col. Charles W. West, one-time resident of Cincinnati. The elder West determined to build a new hotel in Minneapolis. This was the West, at Hennepin Avenue and Fifth Street. Built of brick and marble, ornate in the style of the period, the West Hotel cost $1,500,000, a fabulous figure for those times. For years it was the city's leading hotel and a favorite haunt of visiting theater people.

Today the city has many fine hotels — the Radisson, the Nicollet, the Curtis, the Leamington, the Calhoun Beach, the Sheridan, and others. Like their predecessors, these rank as among the best in the country. Today as in pioneer times the visitor to the city can have a pleasant stay and excellent food at any one of a number of "strangers' houses."

Yesterday

Today

Tomorrow

at the Radisson by H.L.C.

Indians are smart people. They picked out the location around St. Anthony Falls as very attractive long before the white man paid much attention to it. And there's very little doubt that a couple of chiefs sat at a campfire in front of their teepees near St. Anthony Falls many, many moons ago and had powwow.

"Heap fine place," said Chief No. 1, "be big camping ground some day with many teepees." "You said it," replied Chief No. 2. "With wampum," said Chief No. 1, "we build big hotel right here on Seventh Street." He patted the ground. "You said it," replied Chief No. 2. "Call it Radisson," said Chief No. 1, "in honor of Indians' friend Pierre Esprit Sieur de Radisson." "You said it," replied Chief No. 2.

Many, many moons passed. The Village of St. Anthony added teepee after teepee. The name was changed to Minneapolis. On December 15, 1909, the new Hotel Radisson on Seventh Street was opened with a celebration that was one of the most brilliant social events in the history of the city. Today the Radisson is a hotel of unusual distinction with a national reputation for fine food and entertainment.

Preparatory work has already started on the new Radisson Hotel which will include the present building and extend over 200 feet towards Hennepin Avenue with 400 additional rooms, garage facilities, and new lobby and restaurant areas.

This year, Minneapolis celebrates its centennial. And it is appropriate that during this 100th anniversary year, the Radisson has completed plans and will start work on a greater Radisson Hotel to serve the growing Upper Midwest.

Somewhere in the Happy Hunting Grounds are two Indian chiefs with a keen interest in what goes on around here. "This Radisson," says Chief No. 1, "heap wonderful place. And new Radisson, heap big teepee." "You said it," says Chief No. 2.

the Radisson hotel

LABORE ET HONORE

MINNEAPOLIS

Thomas J. Moore, President   Donald E. Clayton, Manager

One hundred years...

a venerable age for man, marks

only the span of youthhood's

years for our city of Minneapolis.

Those of us now participating

in this significant Minneapolis

Centennial celebration hope that

we are contributing to better

and more enjoyable community

living for all our fellow citizens

today, and to a richer, fuller

life for the generations to follow.

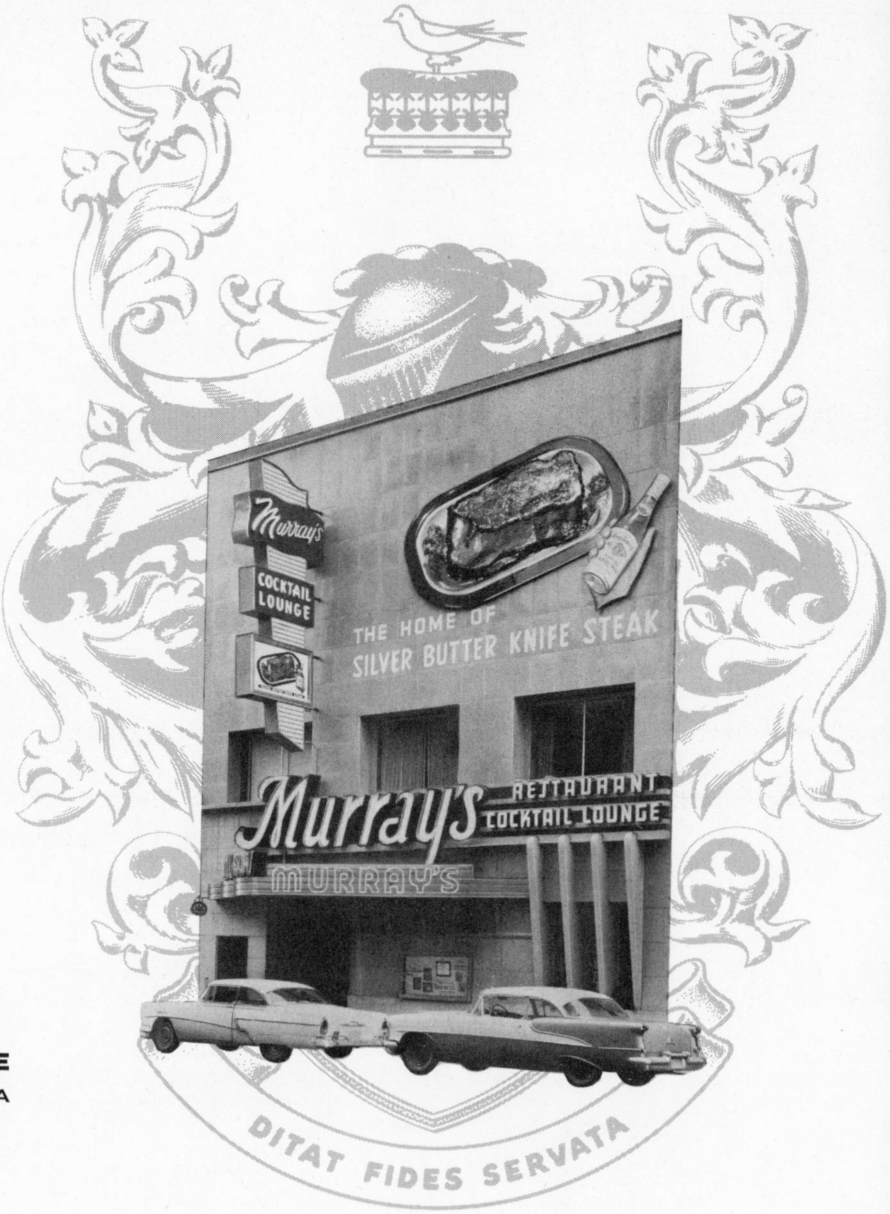

Murray's RESTAURANT AND COCKTAIL LOUNGE
26 SOUTH SIXTH STREET • MINNEAPOLIS, MINNESOTA

TWO DREICER AWARDS
Gold Butter Knife   Silver Butter Knife
Steak Dinner   Steak Dinner

1856

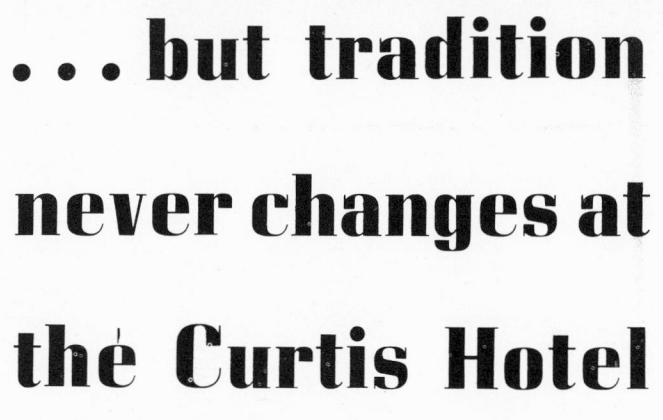

...but tradition never changes at the Curtis Hotel

1956

For over half a century the Curtis Hotel has occupied a traditional place in the ever-changing social and economic scene of Minneapolis ... keeping a sure pace with the growth of the city ... serving its people who have placed a high estimate upon its service and hospitality. Unique it is that, during the five decades since its founding in 1905, the Curtis Hotel has been continually under the direction of three generations of the Melony family. The entire staff offers congratulations to the beautiful Mill City on its 100th anniversary.

The Largest Hotel in the Upper Midwest

The new "Hall of States" Grand Ballroom

Helping Minneapolis off to the right start in a second Century of Progress . . .

HOTEL
Leamington

Hotel Leamington's new two-story addition housing the fabulous "Hall of States" Grand Ballroom on the lobby level, and the new Exhibition and Banquet Hall directly below, gives Minneapolis the largest and finest convention and banquet facilities in the entire Northwest.

The "Hall of States" accommodates up to 3,000 for meetings, 2,000 for banquets. It can also be divided by folding, sound-proof partitions into 7 smaller rooms named for states in our area. The Banquet and Exhibition Hall accommodates over 100 display booths, seats 1450 for meetings or 1,000 for banquets—and can also be quickly divided into smaller rooms. These plus other outstanding features give Hotel Leamington facilities equaled only in a handful of our leading eastern cities!

MAYFAIR RESTAURANT ↑ 35 EXECUTIVE SUITES ↓ NORSE ROOM ↑ 700 KING-SIZED ROOMS ↓

THIRD AVENUE S. BETWEEN 10th and 11th Sts.
Two Parking Lots Adjoining FEderal 3-6161

The fabulous John L. Sullivan, America's first great sports hero, was unbeaten for 10 years. His admirers followed him in the streets.

By 1893 boxing grew popular as a spectator sport, moved uptown, providing the public with the excitement it craved.

Horse racing became a highlight of every county fair. It was utilitarian in that it improved speed and stamina of horses.

Congratulations Minneapolis!

1856 - 1956

ON YOUR CENTENNIAL BIRTHDAY

1856 - 1956 . . . The span of a century, during which a sprawling young settlement grew to a great metropolitan center . . . from early days of pioneering in lumber, sawmills, flour mills, and fur trading, to a great city of industry, finance, education, culture and recreation.

From the days of John L. Sullivan, invincible boxer of the gaslight era, to a modern era of organized recreation in a setting of civic beauty and continuing progress.

We salute you, Minneapolis — we are proud of our citizenship in this great community.

Tempo
bar and restaurant

2027 EAST FRANKLIN, MINNEAPOLIS
TOMMY ANDERSON, Proprietor *

*TOMMY ANDERSON IS PRESIDENT AND MATCHMAKER OF THE MILL CITY BOXING CLUB, INC.

CHOICE BUFFALO STEAKS

BUFFALO STEAKS, venison and wild fowl — these choice items were on the bill o' fare in the newborn city of St. Anthony a hundred years ago.

Today — at Worwa's Cafe, in the heart of Old St. Anthony Village, you will find the world's finest cuisine, served in an atmosphere of liesurely hospitality. You will enjoy your visit to Worwa's.

Skylight Room and Cedar Room Are Available for Party Group

SKYLIGHT ROOM

MAIN DINING ROOM

WORWA'S CAFE

Twenty-three Hundred University Avenue N. E.

Your Hosts: Joe and Don Worwa

Telephone ST. 9-8857

MINNEAPOLIS
Biltmore MOTOR HOTEL
Modern as Tomorrow

Motor travel in the 1907 model at left was a pioneering venture indeed. Motor Hotels for travellers were not even a distant dream.

Today's Biltmore Motor Hotel with its 80 living units sets a new standard for your complete comfort. Never before has a motor hotel been so thoroughly restful. Double walls separate all rooms, so that every room has its own four walls that you share with no one else. What wonderful privacy and peace! Thick carpeted floors, acoustical ceilings and soft furnishings add to the refreshing silence.

The Biltmore Motor Hotel will delight you. It's luxurious-quiet-refreshing-and convenient. Special suites and banquet rooms for parties up to 200 persons. **For reservations, phone WEst 9-8571.**

U.S. HIGHWAYS 169-212

at 52nd STREET S.W.

WEst 9-8571

MINNEAPOLIS, MINNESOTA

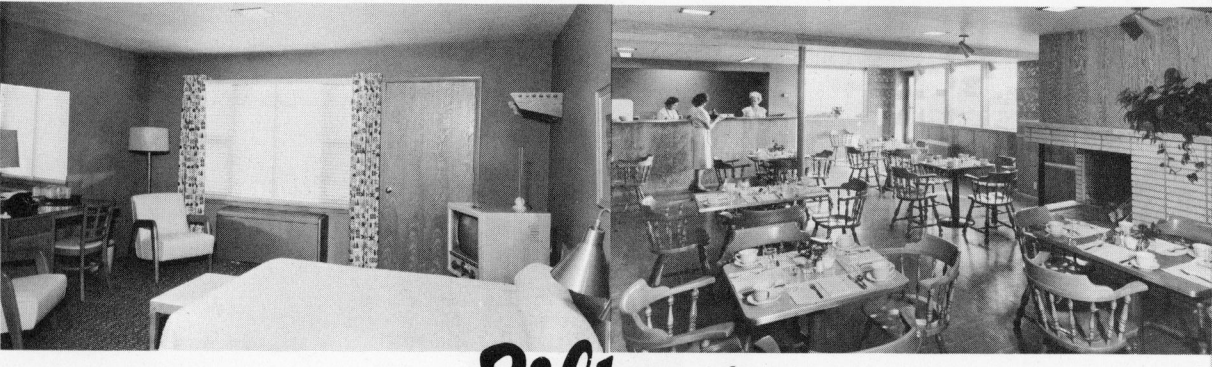

MINNEAPOLIS *Biltmore* MOTOR HOTEL

THE WINSLOW HOUSE

If stone walls could tell tales some exceedingly interesting scraps of history and romance might have been gathered around the old Winslow House. It was the leading hotel of its day and generation, the pride of the natives and the admiration of visitors. It was a fashionable summer rendezvous and, all in all, was one of the wonders of the little world in which the pioneer citizens lived. Its career as a hotel was brilliant but brief. The escape of fugitive slaves and ghost stories galore are among the legacies of its long period of decline and fall. The pioneer Minneapolitan always had a tender spot in his breast for the old Winslow, and witnessed its deliberate destruction with a pang.

. . . we grew with Minneapolis too!

Two shiny, new 1919 Model T Ford touring cars comprised the "fleet" of the first Rent A Car business in the Northwest, founded 37 years ago by Paul Siever. They were stored in Mr. T. B. Walker's Carriage House, on the side of the firm's present location at 5 South 8th Street.

Many a Minneapolis motorist learned to drive in a car rented from this pioneer firm. Subsequently, Siever started a truck leasing business which today is the largest in the Northwest.

Minneapolis Drive Yourself System, Inc., is the name under which the original firm now carries on its extensive car rental operations in Minneapolis and at the Municipal Airport. Since 1924 the firm has been a licensee of the world-wide Hertz System, and has many makes and models of new 1956 automobiles, with "everything furnished but the driver."

We are proud to have had a small part in the development of our fine city since the end of World War I.

Minneapolis Drive Yourself System, Inc.

8th and HENNEPIN

since 1919

FEderal 3-4444

24-hour service

Minneapolis Public Schools

In 1856, the year Minneapolis received its charter, the Minnesota legislature authorized trustees of school district No. 1 in Hennepin county to borrow $10,000. These funds were used to build the Union school on the present site of the courthouse and city hall.

While the opening of the Union school in 1858 with an enrollment of 320 was the big event in early school history on the west side of the river, a notable previous school had been started in St. Anthony in 1851. It was called the Primary school of the University of Minnesota, just incorporated by the territorial legislature.

Early school records are sketchy or nonexistent until 1860, when the first meeting of the Board of Education of the City of St. Anthony was held. The minutes of the board show that the one teacher of the high school in 1860 was paid $35 a month for a term of four months. In the six primary and intermediate schools salaries ranged down to $18 a month for the three-month term.

When St. Anthony was joined with Minneapolis in 1872, the Mississippi river still divided the city schools into two separate systems. There was one school board for the east division and another for the west division. It was the west division which in 1874 built the Adams school, still in use today.

Two significant events occured in 1878. The legislature united the two school boards to form the Board of Education of the City of Minneapolis. And the first high school building was opened. This was Central high school, then located on Third avenue south, between Eleventh and Twelfth streets.

Of the many able men who were superintendents of the Minneapolis public schools the two whose terms were longest deserve particular attention. O. V. Tousley served continuously from 1871 to 1886, the period when the foundations of the present public school system were being laid. His annual reports indicate that he was deeply concerned with making an education available to every child of school age.

Dr. C. M. Jordan, for whom one of the present junior high schools is named, was superintendent from 1892 to 1914. His administration was faced not only with rapid expansion of the school population but also with many changes in the educational program. The minutes of the board, during these years, emphasize the problems of obtaining state aid, of the establishment of kindergartens, and of the introduction of sewing, cooking, manual training and industrial arts into the curriculum.

The Minneapolis Times of September 30, 1896, carried an article with the headlines: "A Boom in Kids — Supt. Jordan Doesn't Know What to Do with Them." The schools which in 1878 had a staff of 98 teachers and enrolled 5,270 pupils now had 769 teachers and 33,673 pupils. At the end of Dr. Jordan's superintendency in 1914 the enrollment had become 49,167, the staff had grown to 1,423 and there were 74 school buildings.

The decade 1920-1930 saw tremendous growth in secondary education in Minne-

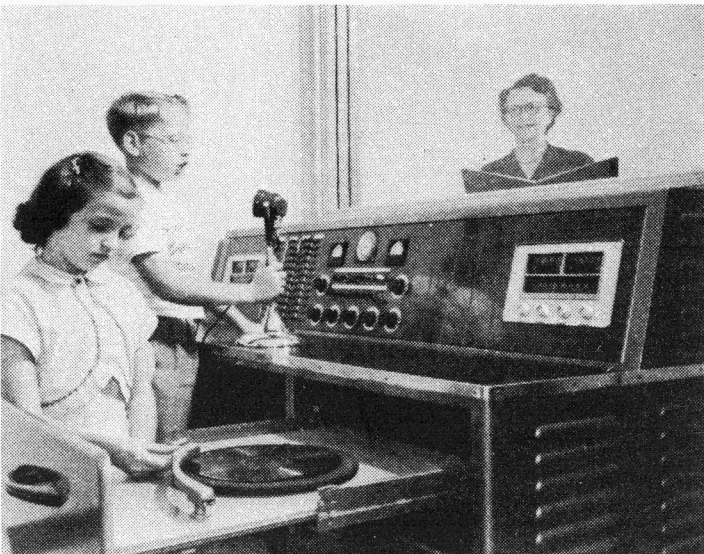

On the opposite page is the old Washington school built in 1865, the second school building in Minneapolis. At upper right is the fifth grade in the Garfield school in 1896. The other three pictures illustrate improved lighting facilities and opportunities now offered for pupil participation in classroom activities.

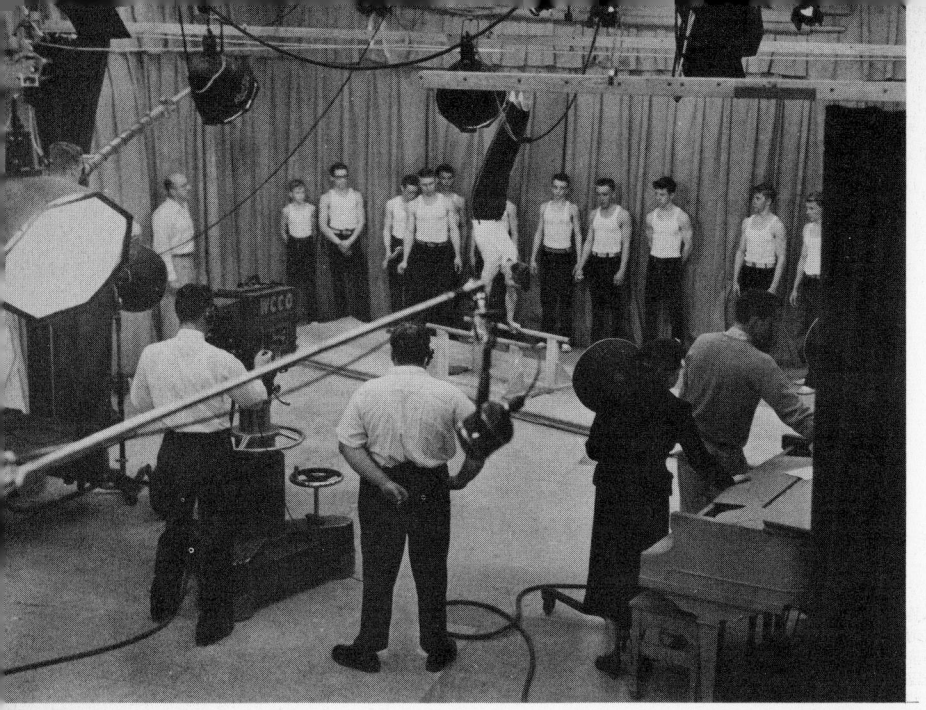

Modern education stresses the all-around development of young people. Physical education is given emphasis as one important phase of a pupil's training. Above, pupils from Roosevelt High School exhibit their prowess on television. Training in home economics is stressed in the high schools. Above, the Home Economics room at South High School. Special training is given in mechanics at Vocational School. Commercial subjects are important courses too (opposite page). Elementary pupils are given frequent opportunities to exhibit their special skills and abilities.

Charles M. Jordan

apolis. In this period 16 of the present 22 junior and senior high schools were either erected or had additions built to them. With this growth in facilities came also a growth in opportunities for service. The Dowling School for Crippled Children was opened in 1920, and previously classes had been established for the blind, the deaf and the mentally retarded. In 1932 the building of Vocational high school gave impetus to the program of trade training and industrial education.

The last decade of Minneapolis' first century has seen the schools take an increasingly important part in community life with the expansion of opportunities for adult education. As the school system begins its second 100 years nearly 70,000 pupils are enrolled in its classes; 2,665 teachers, principals and consultants guide the instruction in its 98 schools, and its annual operating expenditures total approximately 22 million dollars.

ST ANTHONY
HIGH SCHOOL

Rev. F. Tissot
(1866-1887)

Minneapolis Parochial Schools

The first Roman Catholic church in Minneapolis was built in 1849 in St. Anthony village and four years later, in 1853, a parish school was opened in a rented store. The Sisters of St. Joseph were the teachers. By 1866 the church was able to build a schoolhouse.

Father Tissot, pastor of St. Anthony's parish, opened a mission school across the river in what is now the Minneapolis downtown district in 1866. This mission church and school, located near Third Street North and Second Avenue, was the beginning of the present parish of the Basilica of St. Mary, Sixteenth Street and Laurel Avenue. The present school at this new location was built in 1913.

A church for German-speaking Catholics was built in 1858 not far from the Church of St. Anthony at what is now University and Second Street Northeast. This parish also established a mission church across the river in North Minneapolis in 1870. In 1875, the mission church, St. Joseph's, 1162 Fifth Street North, became an independent parish. In that year, 1875, schools were opened in both St. Boniface and St. Joseph's parishes.

As the city developed new parishes were established and new schools opened. At the present time there are thirty-two parish schools with an enrollment of 15,528 students. These schools are staffed by sisters from nine different religious communities,

assisted by fifty-seven teachers. The most recent school built in Minneapolis is St. Kevin's 28th Avenue South and 59th Street, opened in 1952.

St. Anthony's parish school extended instruction beyond the elementary grades and now has a secondary school with 350 girls enrolled. When the mission church of the Immaculate Conception was established on the west bank of the river the Sisters of St. Joseph, in 1877, opened an academy for girls in a house near the parish church.

The academy, called Holy Angels, was first located at Second Street North and Second Avenue. Later it was moved to Fourth Street North and Seventh Avenue. In 1907, when the district was no longer suitable for a girls' school, the students were transferred to the newly opened St. Margaret's Academy, 1301 Linden Avenue.

The property on which St. Margaret's Academy stands was originally purchased as the site for the new Basilica of St. Mary. When this site was judged inadequate for the new church the property was sold to the Sisters of St. Joseph who remodeled the buildings to adapt them for use as a girls' school. The new school was opened in 1907. At the present time St. Margaret's has an enrollment of 419 girls.

In 1900 a school for boys, called the Hennepin Institute, staffed by the Christian Brothers, was opened on Nicollet Island. In 1902 the school was renamed De La Salle High School after the founder of the Christian Brothers.

When the enrollment at the school was so large that all the boys could not be accommodated at the Nicollet Island site a building at Forty-third Street and Wentworth Avenue South was acquired to house the ninth grade. De La Salle School now has an enrollment of 1,200 boys.

In 1931 the Sisters of St. Joseph built a new academy of the Holy Angels at Sixty-sixth Street and Nicollet Avenue. It has an enrollment of 700 young women. There are now four Catholic high schools with 2,671 students. They are taught by 79 teachers in religious orders and 44 laymen.

A City of Churches

Religious activities in the Minneapolis area probably go back as far as the late seventeenth century to the arrival of Father Louis Hennepin at St. Anthony Falls, but formal church organization dates from the early Fort Snelling period.

In 1835 the Rev. J. D. Stevens organized a Presbyterian church at the Fort. He was succeeded by the Rev. Samuel W. Pond, and in 1849 the name of the church was changed to the Oak Grove Presbyterian Church. It was later reorganized as the First Presbyterian Church of Minnesota at Minnehaha.

After the first settlements, church organization in the region was rapid. In 1849 St. Anthony of Padua church, oldest in Minneapolis, was founded by a group of French Canadians under the pioneer priest,

Father Ravoux. The First Congregational Church of St. Anthony was founded in 1851, Gethsemane Episcopal Church in 1856. The history of the Lutheran church in Minneapolis dates back to 1856 also.

Other congregations were established through the 1860's and 1870's. In October, 1878, the first Jewish congregation was organized as Congregation Shaarai Tof. It later became Temple Israel.

Today there are more than 420 churches in Minneapolis, representing practically all religious faiths. Many of them are of outstanding architectural beauty. Some, such as St. Francis Cabrini Catholic Church, Lake Harriet Methodist Church, and the Lutheran Church of the Good Shepherd are striking examples of modern architecture.

As modern as tomorrow is the Lake Harriet Methodist Church (on opposite page at extreme left) Front entrance of St. Mark's Cathedral and its main structure (on opposite page) which has been a Minneapolis landmark since 1910. Where Hennepin Avenue curves out of the business district to the south stands the Basilica of St. Mary, shrine of the Roman Catholic faith. (at upper left) An outstanding example of modern functional architecture is the Catholic church of St. Frances Cabrini (at lower right). The other two pictures are of Central Lutheran Church, with the largest seating capacity of any church in Minneapolis.

At upper left is the new structure of the First Christian Church and at lower right is the new St. Olaf Catholic Church, designed by Thorshov and Cerny. Below is the Gothic-styled Mount Olivet Lutheran Church, a building completed in 1949 to accommodate one of the fastest growing congregations in the city.

At upper left is Hennepin Avenue Methodist Church whose needle-like spire is visible for miles. At upper right is Plymouth Congregational Church organized in 1857. At lower center is Westminster Presbyterian Church organized before 1883. Below, Gethsemane Episcopal Church organized in 1856. At lower left, the interior of Second Church of Christ Scientist.

A Center of Food Processing

Situated as it is in the very heart of a rich agricultural area, Minneapolis has developed into a food processing center. World known for its brand breakfast foods produced by such firms as Cream of Wheat Corporation, Malt-o-Meal Co., Pillsbury Mills, and General Mills, Minneapolis has created new methods for food preservation and storage. Not only have the food needs of local consumers been satisfied by a vast array of varied processing concerns, but they have served millions of people in a seven-state trade area. From the pioneer days of a century ago up to the present time, man's ingenuity has been constantly utilized to furnish tasty food to please the palate of the most fastidious gourmet.

"GOLDEN CHIPS"

GOLDEN POTATO CHIPS, flavored to the peak of perfection, roll off the spotless conveyors at the Old Dutch Kitchens in a continuous golden stream, on their way to the tables of hundreds of thousands of Northwest citizens, who relish these crispy delicacies from Minnesota.

Old Dutch Potato Chips are made from the finest potatoes from the fertile Red River Valley by Old Dutch's unique food process and delivered fresh to your table with the flavor sealed in.

In early years caravans of Red River Ox carts brought these lush products from the Red River Valley to St. Anthony Falls, distributing point for all points of the compass.

Today, Old Dutch Foods, with its most modern food processing equipment takes pride in its Minneapolis citizenship, and the part it has been able to play in the city's development as a Food Processing Center.

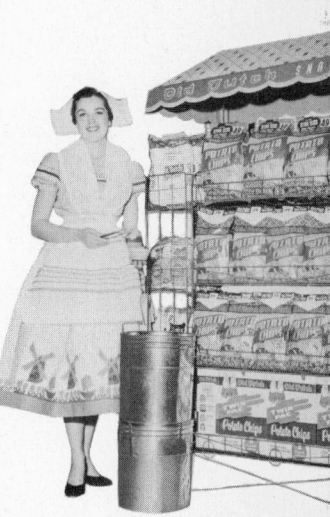

HERE'S THE STORY IN A NUT SHELL:

FOUNDED IN 1933.
Annual Sales (banked in Minneapolis) $2,500,000.
Annual Payroll (spent in Minneapolis) $ 544,325.

PLANS FOR THE FUTURE:
Governed only by our ability to meet the ever-growing demand for Old Dutch Food Products.

Old Dutch Foods

MINNEAPOLIS, MINNESOTA

In 100 years...

Boys and Milk really haven't changed

...but they're handled better now!

Boys are the same today as when Minneapolis was young. But today's boy can expect to live more than 25 years longer!

Part of the credit for longer life, better health and stronger teeth is due to milk . . . and the safeguards of modern handling methods.

Twin City Milk Producers Association was formed to efficiently handle and market the milk of dairy farmers in the Twin City area . . . and to serve the consuming public by supplying bottling plants with an adequate supply of pure and wholesome milk each day.

We have grown and progressed with Minneapolis from a humble beginning. Today, 5,000 dairy farmers—who milk 80,000 cows—supply the Twin City area with almost 20 million quarts of fresh milk per month, handled and processed in the finest dairy equipment.

Yes, growing boys in Minneapolis today (and their sisters and parents, too) are assured of having all the wholesome fresh milk they want at reasonable prices . . . due to the efficient and modern way in which milk is marketed in the Twin City area.

TWIN CITY MILK 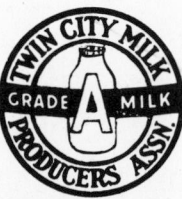 PRODUCERS ASSN.

Serving Metropolitan Minneapolis-St. Paul   *with fresh Grade "A" Milk.*

A Salute

TO THE GREAT CITY OF MINNEAPOLIS

On its 100ᵗʰ Birthday

1856 — 1956

We at the Coca-Cola Bottling Company are proud to be a part of the modern, pace-setting, ever expanding metropolis that is the CITY OF MINNEAPOLIS.

We salute and congratulate its citizens who are our neighbors and friends who, through the years, have made Minneapolis **their** city and **ours**, one of America's greatest!

We are proud too, to point out the location of our modern plant as the historic site where once stood the nationally famous Exposition Building—focal point of the social, cultural, civic and political life of the youthful enterprising city of Minneapolis

From its halls evolved the many ideas for growth, dreams of greatness, plans for a city among cities—all to be realized in this, its Centennial year of 1956.

1886—THE YEAR COCA-COLA WAS BORN

Minneapolis Exposition Building Erected in 1886

The Coca-Cola plant on the former Exposition Building site

THE COCA-COLA BOTTLING COMPANY

The Gluek Brewing Co. — 100 years ago

MINNE was the word for water
...GLUEK the word for beer

Minneapolis got its name from a coined or made-up word. To Minne, the Sioux word for water, they added Apolis, the Greek word for city. And Gluek was the word for beer when Minneapolis was officially born 100 years ago.

Today, the Gluek brewery stands on the banks of the Mississippi where the first Gluek brewery stood a century ago. The men of Gluek have seen the birth of Minneapolis and have seen it grow.

They have watched the skyline change. They have seen ways of living and ways of pleasure change. But for many, many thousands of people, Gluek still is the word for beer. It still is the beer that belongs where good friends meet and hearts are gay.

GLUEK BREWING CO., MPLS., MINN.

Our 100th Year
GLUEK

Proud symbol of a century-old brewing heritage

ATWOOD'S COFFEE SINCE 1902

Minneapolitans have enjoyed Atwood Coffee since 1902, the year that J. F. Atwood and his brother Eben Atwood established their business. This company pioneered in the process of roasting and blending coffee beans imported green from Central and South America.

Today, the aromatic goodness of each delicious cup of Atwood Coffee is a tribute to the years of Atwood experience in every step of an exacting process — roasting, blending, grinding, packaging and distributing to the consumer, with the flavor sealed in.

The Minneapolis story is the Atwood story, a story of growth and expansion, and of pride in service to the people who make our area what it is — a fine community in which to live. Our salute to Minneapolis on its hundredth birthday!

Eben Atwood
Founder

Henry M. Atwood
President

J. F. Atwood
Founder

THE ATWOOD COFFEE COMPANY

The Atwood Coffee Company supplies a critical clientele in the hotel, restaurant, and retail grocery trade. Its territory includes Minnesota, Wisconsin, Iowa, upper Michigan, North Dakota, South Dakota, and Montana.

Frontier Treat

Our frontier farmers cooled their mi
pans or earthen crocks, in a dugout

Today, milk production and distrib
The fresh Grade A milk you enjoy
cows on over 4,000 farms surroundi

Modern dairy farms . . . refrigera

MINNEAPOLIS

nilk...

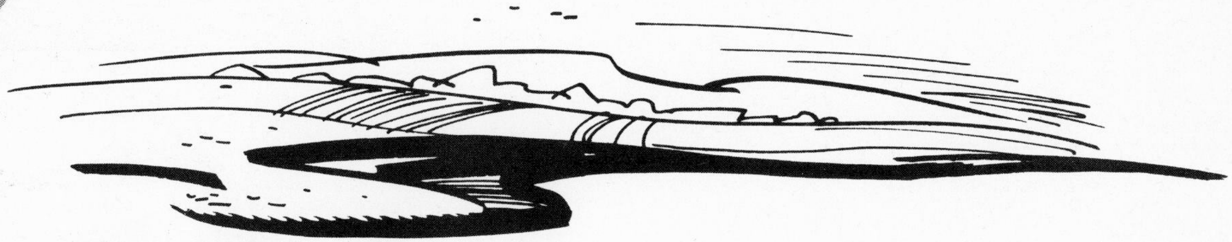

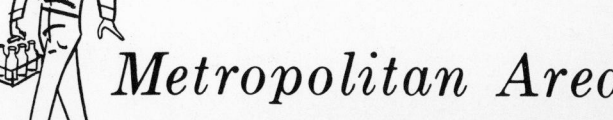

When Minneapolis Was Young

a dozen cows in open

rm a vast industry.
ced by some 80,000
win Cities.

less steel tanks for

rapid cooling . . . a huge fleet of trucks . . . efficient bottling plants . . . all have made fresh, fluid milk a dependable, low-cost food and beverage.

To many, the milk industry is a friendly man with a wire basket. But between Bossy and your milkman is an investment of millions in equipment and service. Milk . . . and Minneapolis . . . have kept pace with progress!

IILK DISTRIBUTORS

. . . Serving A Great Metropolitan Area

...an' have yez ever heard th' story of Maggie O' Rooney?

WELL SOR, y'see it wuz this way . . .

Many years ago a foine broth 'v a man b' the name of Pat O' Rooney lived in Ireland but a stone's throw from Dublin. His good wife Maggie, ah, now there wuz a woman fer yez, brightened up his days as well as th' tidy little cottage b' th' side of the road.

Wan day without a word of warnin', Pat came down wid a painful ailmint in the region 'v th' stomach. Bein' a robust man he wuz vexed to be so afflicted. Shure the doctors came an' divil of a cure could they find at all, at all. So, Maggie wid her wise little smile an' her deft little hands went to work fixin' a batch of dough, kneadin' it tenderly an' delicately, then rollin' it into long thin strings. Then she dried 'em an' cooked 'em and fed 'em to her husband, Pat.

Well, glory be, 'tis th' gospel truth, Pat began to get well. Th' neighbors swore it wor a Miracle, so they did, an' wid Maggie's recipe they started makin' an' servin' the delicacies an' callin' them "Margaret O'Rooneys" after Pat's wife.

Then a restaurant in Dublin started servin' th' tasty dish an' wan day an Italian trav'ler feastin' at the restaurant excitedly wrote down the recipe an' took it back to Italy. Lo an' behold, he started his own restaurant an' featured "Margaret O'Rooney". Like most 'v them furriners he niver could pronounce good Irish names, so to this day all of Italy eats Maggie's creation under the name 'v macaroni.

So, y' see, macaroni is a native product 'v th' Emerald Isle an' don't be lettin' anybody ever tell yez diffrunt!

This tale, attributed to Mr. James T. Williams, founder of The Creamette Company, shows that there was some relaxation from the work of establishing a macaroni products business in Minneapolis. And it's the same alert outlook that has today expanded the Company's activities into frozen ready-to-bake macaroni dishes and frozen pancake batter . . . just as in its early days, this Company originated Creamettes—the tender, thin-walled, quick cooking macaroni . . . the short curved lengths of ready-cut spaghetti.

And it is this spirit that continues to maintain The Creamette Company as truly representative of the progressive industries of Minneapolis.

100 years OF PROGRESS

The growth of Minneapolis, the growth of her people and her industry are so interdependent and entwined they are synonomous. The growth of Minneapolis as a market and a vast resource of human skills and knowledge has provided industry with the food for growth. And Minneapolis industry, in its turn, has realized its great responsibility to its people. It has been in this atmosphere of progress and partnership that Minneapolis has lived and grown her first hundred years.

Throughout these years, Minneapolis Brewing Company has grown with the city. Times have changed, methods have changed, markets have changed. The Minneapolis Brewing Company looks forward to the next 100 years of progress with the same enthusiasm and faith in the future that our founders displayed nearly a century ago.

MINNEAPOLIS BREWING COMPANY

MINNEAPOLIS, MINNESOTA

MINNEAPOLIS—
Distribution Center

Necessary commodities reached the early settlers of this area by way of riverboat and oxcart. Because of a strategic location in the heart of a rich agricultural territory, our city was destined to become a great distribution and jobbing center comparable to its foremost position as a world wheat market center. Railroad transportation developed and the pioneer merchants of the city became the first jobbers and suppliers.

Among the early wholesale distributors were: Janney, Semple & Co., hardware; Forman, Ford & Co., glass; Wyman, Partridge & Co., dry goods; Thurber & Co., furniture; James H. Bishop & Co., paper; George R. Newell & Co., groceries; Deere & Co., implements.

Minneapolis has continued since the early days to maintain its standing as a jobbing center. At the end of its first century the dollar total of the products distributed has totaled many millions and the volume continues to rise.

Portrait of progress!

The Portrait of Progress is an ever changing scene! A century ago Minneapolis citizens erected the first bridge to span the Mississippi anywhere—an effort that brought a major change to the simple portrait of Minneapolis, 1856!

Just a decade later, Janney and Moles began a small hardware business near that bridge. Their effort, modest as it was, became the foundation of an organization that has earned a prominent place in the great portrait of progress that is Minneapolis, 1956!

Today the firm of Janney, Semple, Hill and Company is in its 90th year. It has grown from a small store on a dirt street to a gigantic distributor of fine quality hardware in 22 states, Alaska and Canada. And—in keeping with the March of Progress—Janney, Semple, Hill and Company serves a progressive group of independent hardware retailers known as the SERVICE & QUALITY HARDWARE STORES with every facility needed to put them on an equal footing with chain store competitors.

The Portrait of Progress is an ever changing scene! Tomorrow's portrait will be even more impressive. And Janney, Semple, Hill and Company will play an important part in it—seeking and supplying new wants and needs of an ever advancing populace—distributing the best products American industry can produce.

1866

JANNEY, SEMPLE, HILL & CO.
MINNEAPOLIS, MINNESOTA

In the Minneapolis Tradition...

PROGRESS through INDEPENDENCE

First Hardware Store in Minnesota Territory.
Drawing from original photograph, courtesy
of Minnesota Historical Society

He was going to be his own boss for a change! He was going up there in the new Minnesota Territory and open a hardware store and be his own man. Figured he'd do all right, too.

And he did. In 1853 he opened the first hardware store in Minnesota Territory... that was three years before Minneapolis was even a city. He didn't have inviting window displays, or a great range of merchandise. But he had what pioneer people needed. And they bought from him, and he did just fine.

You look through any one of the 567 Our Own Hardware Stores today and there doesn't seem to be much connection between it and that first hardware store. Hardware . . . real hardware . . . hammers, saws, axes and things like that are just a small part of what you find. But when you take a long look, the likeness is there. You notice it in two big things. First, the store owner is independent; he's his own man. Second, the things he sells are right in step with what his people need. Progress through independence, we call it, and it works as well today as it did a century ago.

The 567 OUR OWN HARDWARE DEALERS
who own Our Own Hardware Company

Inside and outside ...

Since 1883 ...

Minnesota hospitality has been built into the most beautiful Twin City homes and the
most successful, progressive businesses with Forman, Ford glass and Forman, Ford paint.
Your home and your business will benefit by the advice and help of competent Forman,
Ford consultants—men who *know* glass and *know* paint.

Their services are free and as close as FEderal 3-4301.

FORMAN FORD & CO.

111 SOUTH 2ND STREET · MINNEAPOLIS 1, MINNESOTA

50,000 square feet of glass

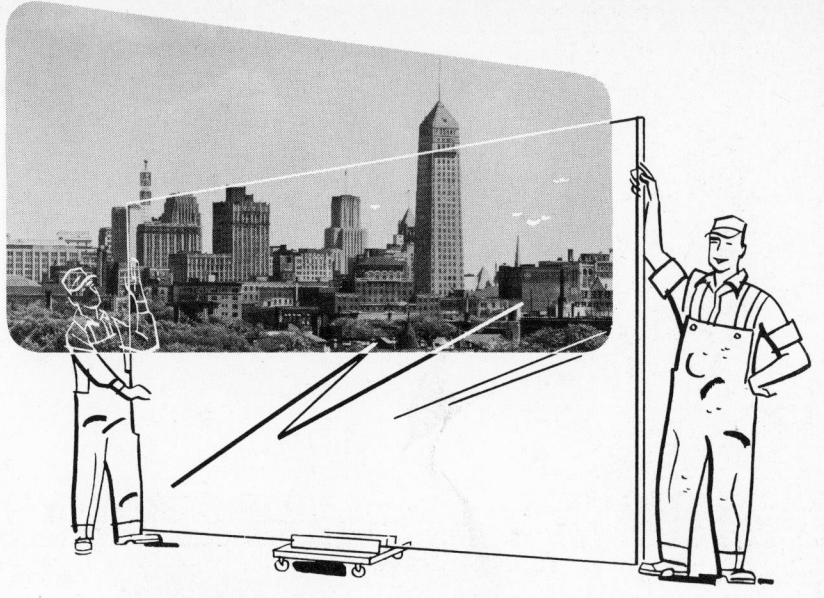

This was the amount of polished plate glass that Northwestern Glass Company installed during 1955 in new Minneapolis structures.

Glass has been our business in Minneapolis for fifty years! This important building material requires perfection in handling, with highly specialized equipment for its transportation and installation. This company is recognized as a leader in its field and has customers, both small and large, throughout Minnesota and adjoining states. Among the large-scale glazing jobs in Minneapolis have been the Rand Tower, Baker and Roanoke Buildings, and the Nicollet Hotel.

We join our city with pride in her centennial celebration, and with grateful appreciation for the opportunities we have been given to share in the building and growth of our great metropolis.

EMIL C. KISCHEL,
Founder

O. A. FEUDNER,
Manager

The same personnel has been active in the management of the company almost since its founding in 1907 — including O. A. Feudner, R. M. Mulholland, H. M. Carroll, and Miss O. V. Nordstrom.

NORTHWESTERN GLASS COMPANY

219 - 223 NORTH SECOND STREET • MINNEAPOLIS

HOME OF
Gamble Skogmo

AT HOME in MINNEAPOLIS
SINCE 1928

It's a good life. Good for business—good for the people who live and work here. That's why Minneapolis now flourishes as a business and cultural center for this vast trade region. Gamble-Skogmo has been "at home" in Minneapolis since 1928, growing with the city, and helping it grow. Starting as just one small store in the midwest, it now is a family of over 2100 company and dealer-owned stores throughout central and western United States and Canada. With our home office and a central warehouse located right here in Minneapolis, we're pleased and mighty proud that we have been part of Minneapolis' illustrious past—part of her great future—glad to be "at home" in Minneapolis.

Gamble-Skogmo, Inc.   15 North Eighth Street, Minneapolis 3

E. L. Carpenter

Minneapolis Symphony Orchestra

The story of music in Minneapolis goes a long way back — to military bands at old Fort Snelling, to the singing Hutchinson family in territorial days, to the early singing clubs in the new city, to Ole Bull and the young Adelina Patti—but it all comes to a focus in one of the city's greatest and most famous assets, the Minneapolis Symphony Orchestra.

Now under the direction of young, dynamic Antal Dorati the orchestra has had a distinguished line of conductors, two of whom, Eugene Ormandy and Dimitri Mitropoulos, have gone on to national and international fame.

There had been earlier orchestras in Minneapolis, some of them of considerable merit though not of symphony caliber, but it was not until 1903 that the Minneapolis

Symphony took form. Emil Oberhoffer, a Bavarian who had come to the Twin Cities in the 1890's, was the first conductor. The orchestra's debut was in the old Exposition Building on the east side of the river.

E. L. Carpenter, a young lumberman with an almost professional interest in music, was a moving spirit of the development of the orchestra. When the Orchestral Association of Minneapolis was incorporated at the beginning of the fifth season in 1907, Carpenter was elected president, a position he held until his death in 1945.

Very early in its career, the Minneapolis Symphony became a traveling orchestra. In 1907 it played concerts in Duluth, Grand Forks and Moorhead. In the 49 years that have passed since then the orchestra has traveled all over the United States and

Canada and has visited Cuba. Its journeys have given it a well deserved national reputation.

In 1905 the Symphony moved into the Auditorium, now the Lyceum Theater, which was to remain its home for the next quarter century. In 1914 the Symphony began duplicating its Friday night concerts in Minneapolis on Thursday nights in St. Paul. The St. Paul concerts were abandoned when the Symphony formed an association with the University of Minnesota and moved to Northrop Auditorium on the main campus in 1930.

After a 19-year reign over the orchestra, Emil Oberhoffer resigned in 1922. In the following season the Symphony had five guest conductors, Bruno Walter, Walter Damrosch, Albert Coates, Ossip Gabrilo-

witsch and Henri Verbrugghen. Verbrugghen, a Belgian musician who had been conducting in Australia, was announced as the new permanent conductor.

At the beginning of the 1931 season, after the Symphony had moved to the University, Verbrugghen was taken sick. Mrs. Carlyle Scott, who had taken over management of the orchestra, was faced with the difficult job of finding a conductor when season schedules were already well fixed. She found him in young Eugene Ormandy, who was to go on from Minneapolis to be associate conductor and then musical director of the Philadelphia Orchestra.

Ormandy moved on to Philadelphia in 1936 and for a time the Minneapolis podium was filled by a succession of guest conductors. Minneapolis concertgoers first saw and heard Mitropoulos in the winter of 1937. A Greek, a mountain climber, and a man of profound religious thought, Mitropoulos was to leave his mark on the cultural life of the city. The reaction of his first Minneapolis audience was immediate and enthusiastic.

Mitropoulos played his last concert as Minneapolis conductor in the spring of 1949, and the following autumn the youthful Antal Dorati, formerly conductor of the Dallas Symphony, took over.

Through the 53 years of its existence the Symphony has had the proud and loyal support of the city. Not only music lovers, but the city's corporations, civic organizations, school children, housewives and laborers have contributed to its support. A Women's Association of the Minneapolis Symphony Orchestra has told the symphony story far and wide over Minnesota, acting as a kind of general public relations organization and incidentally collecting funds for the orchestra through its "chain luncheons."

Probably no one thing has done more for the cultural reputation of Minneapolis than the Symphony. Through its far-ranging tours and its phonograph records, made for RCA-Victor, Columbia, and more recently for Mercury, it has become known to millions of Americans. People in far corners of the world, who know nothing else of Minneapolis (except, possibly, that it mills flour), have heard of the Minneapolis Symphony Orchestra and have respect for it as one of the great musical organizations of the United States.

Transportation

As a city expands, it has growing demands for better and faster transportation. First reached by canoe after months of arduous travel through the wilderness, the village of St. Anthony grew into the Minneapolis of today which is only a few hours away from any point on the earth by air. Wold Chamberlain Field is served by six airlines and handles a volume of air traffic that ranks it seventh in the nation. Ten trunk line railroads, four of which are transcontinental, come into the city. In addition there are five bus companies, 120 motor freight carriers, and 25 barge lines on the Mississippi serving Minneapolis.

196

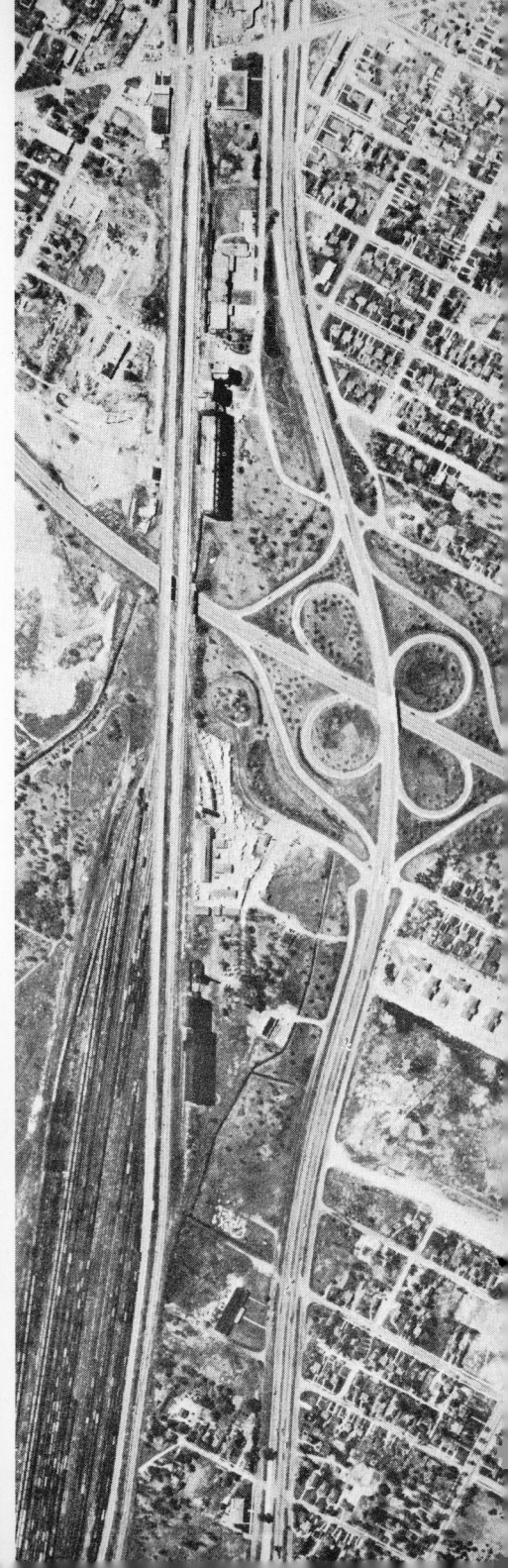

The Milwaukee Streamliner above contrasts sharply with the architecture
of the Milwaukee Station as it appeared in the 80's.

How the Air Age came to Minneapolis

Today, and every day of 1956, hundreds of persons will board Northwest Orient Airlines planes at Wold-Chamberlain and settle back to watch the world skim by below.

Some will fly with us to Chicago—others to New York. Vacationers will take the westbound Strato-cruisers to Seattle or Portland; then fly on with us to Hawaii . . . arriving in less than one day after leaving Minneapolis. Many travelers will fly NWA to Alaska, Japan, Formosa, the Philippine Islands, or the British crown colony of Hongkong.

From water to land to air

This year, as Minneapolis celebrates its hundredth birthday, the journeys of bygone days will be remembered. First, the voyageurs in fragile canoes. Then horses and wagons, laboring slowly overland. Then ribbons of rails and the "iron horse." More recently, the horseless carriage. And 1926, when the air age dawned in Minneapolis.

On October 1, 1926, Northwest made its first commercial flight. One OX-5 open cockpit airplane—half of our total fleet at that time—took off for Chicago with a load of mail. In 1927, we started carrying passengers—106 persons in that first late-summer season.

Then, month by month and city by city, the Northwest line pushed westward. On December 4, 1933, Northwest made an historic flight over the Rocky and Cascade mountains to Seattle; and that city became our western continental terminus.

In the last 30 years, Northwest's certificated routes have grown from 400 to 18,000 miles, now covering more than half the globe. Today, this Twin City-based airline operates several hundred scheduled flights a week — from New York, Washington, D.C. and major cities westward. Our Alaska-Orient flights follow the great circle northern route, shortest and fastest to the Orient, also pioneered by Northwest. This year NWA will fly more than *one billion* passenger-miles.

Thus, in less than one-third of the hundred years since Minneapolis was born, Wold-Chamberlain airport has become a major travel and transport center. Many thousands of loyal Twin Citians have helped bring this about, by support for Northwest Orient Airlines and other air operations centered here.

Today . . . we invest in the future

NWA now has a new $45,000,000 fleet of airliners building. Deliveries will begin this year, bringing us the finest multi-engine planes that money can buy. Jet aircraft, too, are on the way.

On land adjoining Wold-Chamberlain, our new $15,000,000 maintenance base and home office is soon to be built. This installation will express, as nothing else could, our thanks to all our friends and neighbors here, and our faith in the future of this community.

NORTHWEST
Orient AIRLINES

Building with the Twin Cities for the New Air Age

The going is always great in a FORD V-8

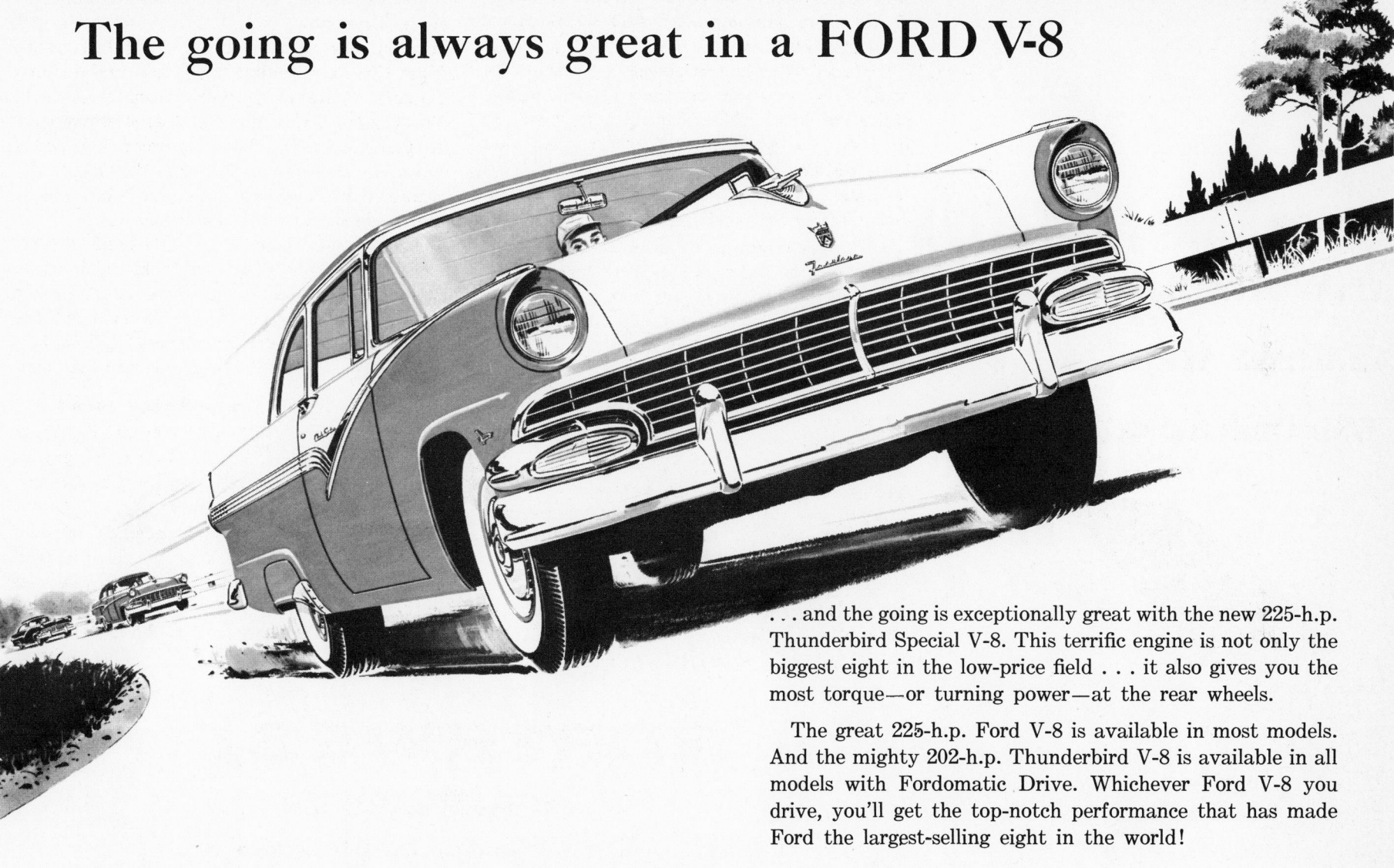

...and the going is exceptionally great with the new 225-h.p. Thunderbird Special V-8. This terrific engine is not only the biggest eight in the low-price field ... it also gives you the most torque—or turning power—at the rear wheels.

The great 225-h.p. Ford V-8 is available in most models. And the mighty 202-h.p. Thunderbird V-8 is available in all models with Fordomatic Drive. Whichever Ford V-8 you drive, you'll get the top-notch performance that has made Ford the largest-selling eight in the world!

SEE YOUR FORD DEALER

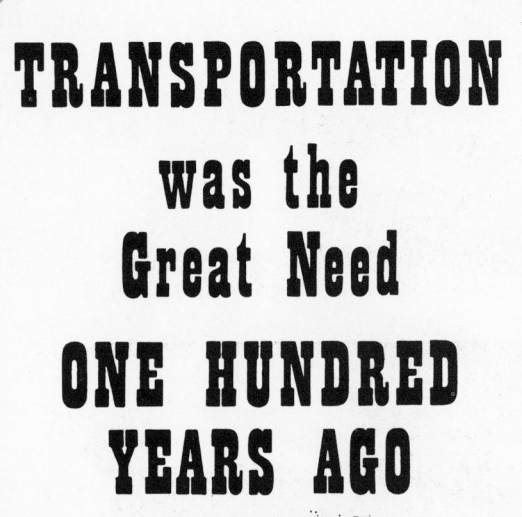

TRANSPORTATION
was the Great Need
ONE HUNDRED YEARS AGO

Early Minneapolis in 1856 had only the Modes of Transportation—boats and horses—known to Washington, Napoleon and the Caesars of Ancient Rome.

In 1862, the First Railroad came to

MINNEAPOLIS

to change the life of the Community

THE SOO LINE RAILROAD

came in 1883

and its coming hastened by many years the Growth and Progress of Minneapolis and the entire Northwest.

"The Soo Road is the grandest enterprise for these two cities ever conceived," wrote H. T. Welles, pioneer business and public leader, who came to St. Anthony in 1853.

THE SOO LINE

An asset to Minneapolis for 73 Years of the Century

MAGNIFICENT POSSESSION...

Behold a bit of tomorrow . . . in the Starfire styling, the double-duty beauty of the ultra-smart "Intagrille Bumper", the lavish luxury of "Fashion-First" interior decor . . . exclusively yours in this

OLDSMOBILE NINETY-EIGHT FOR '56

You'll find Oldsmobile sets standards for the future in power and performance, too, with the mighty Rocket T-350 Engine and Jetaway Hydra-Matic*. So meet magnificent motoring . . . at your Oldsmobile dealer's now.

*Standard on Series Ninety-Eight; optional at extra cost on all other series.

Minnehaha Falls, retained with all its original rugged beauty, continues to be a tourist attraction in summer and winter.

For over half a century, the statue of Ole Bull has played the violin silently over Loring Park.

Out where Wayzata Boulevard meets Cedar Lake Road . . .

. . . the Standard Oil Company is building its ultra-modern new Northwestern Regional Offices which will also house the important Twin Cities Division. It is only proper that this visible evidence of faith in the future of Minneapolis should take form in the year of the Centennial. For Standard Oil has been serving the people of this community with fine petroleum products for more than 62 years.

Approximately 100,000 sq. ft. of space . . . Two stories high with provision for an additional floor . . . Made of steel, concrete, Mankato stone and brick . . . Fully air-conditioned . . . Beautifully landscaped.

The Big Exclusive

To safeguard the quality of the products we provide the people of Minneapolis, Standard Oil owns and operates its own *exclusive* Twin Cities terminal. No gasolines go in or out of this terminal but STANDARD Gasolines —and they go only to Standard customers.

The new offices will provide more than 500 residents of the Twin Cities area with steady, profitable employment in pleasant, healthful surroundings. It is our hope that, as Minneapolis grows we shall too, and contribute even more to the happiness and security of its citizens.

STANDARD

STANDARD OIL COMPANY

MINNEAPOLIS
Insurance Center

In recent years many people have commenced referring to Minneapolis as "the Hartford of the West." The city is gaining a national reputation as an insurance center.

Three years after the city was born, the first Minneapolis directory, in 1859, listed nine insurance agents (there were 19 blacksmiths); today fifty insurance companies maintain regional or home offices here and the Twin Cities now constitute the seventh largest insurance center in America with more than $7,500,000,000 of life insurance in force.

Northwestern National Life of Minneapolis was founded in 1885 and is now the sixth largest life insurance company with home offices west of the Mississippi river. Minnesota Farmers Mutual opened its doors in 1891, and North American Life and Casualty and Austin Mutual in 1896. American Hardware Mutual and Northwestern Fire & Marine were both launched in 1899. Minneapolis Fire & Marine was organized in 1902.

Minneapolis is one of five cities chosen by Prudential Insurance Company, the nation's largest life insurance company, for one of its regional headquarters. The North Central office of Prudential is located here in a beautiful, modern office building—one of the fine landmarks of the city—on Wayzata Boulevard.

Local headquarters of insurance companies have done much in recent years to beautify Minneapolis. The Lutheran Brotherhood Building at Seventh Street and Second Avenue South, is a distinguished addition to the downtown skyline. The Ministers' Life and Casualty Union Building at Lake Street and Excelsior Boulevard is another city asset. American Hardware Mutual has a fine new home in the magnificent setting on the shores of Lake Calhoun. North American Life & Casualty Company has one of America's most modern office buildings at 1750 Hennepin Avenue.

Life insurance companies with headquarters or regional offices in Minneapolis include Prudential, Lutheran Brotherhood, Ministers' Life & Casualty Union, North American Life and Casualty, Northwestern National Life Insurance Company, Standard American Life and State Progressive Life.

Fire and casualty companies here are American Benefit Association, American

General Insurance Company, American Merchants Mutual Insurance Company, Austin Mutual Fire Insurance Company, Austin Mutual Insurance Company, Farmer's Cooperative Mutual Insurance Association, Farmer's Home Mutual Insurance Company, Great Northern Insurance Company, American Hardware Mutual Insurance Company, Minneapolis Fire & Marine Insurance Company, Minnesota Commercial Mens Association, Minnesota Mutual Fire & Casualty Insurance Company, Minnesota Farmer's Mutual Insurance Company, North American Life and Casualty Company, Northern Mutual Insurance Company, Northwestern Farmers Mutual Insurance Company, Northwestern Fire & Marine Insurance Company, Progressive Mutual Assurance Company, Title Insurance Company of Minnesota and Twin City Fire Insurance Company.

205

NORTH AMERICAN
insures
confident
living

North American insurance builds estates, pays off mortgages, helps cover hospital and doctor bills, supplies disability income, makes retirement years fun. It lifts your worries—gives you the peace of mind that lets you step out and enjoy confident living.

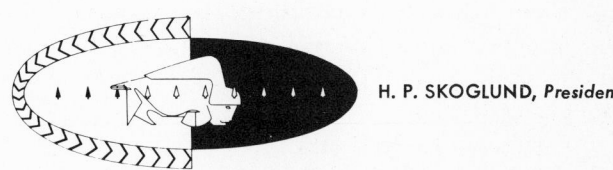

H. P. SKOGLUND, *President*

NORTH AMERICAN
Life and Casualty Company

1750 HENNEPIN AVENUE

1896 • SIXTIETH ANNIVERSARY • 1956

Hats off to the past...
Coats off to the future!

From a pioneer village in 1856 to a great metropolis of the Upper Midwest in 1956—that's the story of Minneapolis. Yet in paying much deserved respect to the men and women who contributed to this Century of Progress in Minneapolis, we are reminded that they built well because their eyes were on the future, not the past.

Our hats are off to those who made the city we know. And our coats are off to help make its future even brighter.

Since establishment of our first Minneapolis office in 1888, Prudential's Rock of Gibraltar has become a familiar symbol of strength and security to more than three million policyholders in the North Central region. And throughout those 68 years, Prudential dollars have been plowed back into the community—encouraging the growth of industry, agriculture and home building.

So it was as an old friend and neighbor that the Prudential selected Minneapolis as the site of its new regional headquarters. Our North Central Home Office is our vote of confidence in Minneapolis as she begins her second hundred years.

THE FUTURE BELONGS TO THOSE WHO PREPARE FOR IT

The PRUDENTIAL
Insurance Company of America

North Central Home Office
Minneapolis, Minnesota

We've moved to Calhoun Knoll

This summer, after 57 years of steady business growth, American Hardware Mutual is formally dedicating its new national headquarters building on Calhoun Knoll—where Excelsior Boulevard meets the parkway at Lake Calhoun.

In the neighborly tradition of moving day—and the spirit of the Minneapolis Centennial—may we introduce ourselves again to old friends and new? First, we are truly a Minneapolis company, founded here and operated here since 1899. Until last year, you knew us as "Hardware Mutual of Minnesota." In April, 1955, to signify our nation-wide service to 230,000 policyholders in 48 states, we changed our name to American Hardware Mutual Insurance Company.

The product we sell is fire and casualty insurance for business, home and automobile. We are a *mutual* company—which, as a matter of record, means lower-cost insurance for everyone we serve. Last year alone, our dividends returned to policyholders reached a record high of more than $4,700,000.

We are proud indeed to have been a part of Minneapolis for 57 of its first 100 years. Now, in our fine new building, we have every needed facility for even better and faster insurance service, and for continued expansion in the years that lie ahead.

Our steady growth *reflects this impressive fact: 50 insurance companies with home offices or major branches here, and 15,000 local employees, have now made the Twin Cities the 7th largest insurance center in the country.*

AMERICAN HARDWARE MUTUAL INSURANCE COMPANY

Insurance for business, home and automobile . . . at lower cost

WE'VE SAID GOODBYE to our former home office building at 24th and Nicollet, which we first occupied in 1923. All our operations will now be carried on from our new building at Calhoun Knoll, 3033 Excelsior Boulevard.

Assets you won't find in our financial statement

Lutheran Brotherhood's most important assets are people . . . their faith, integrity, goodwill and their spirit. Of course we can't include them in our financial statement, but we'd like to acknowledge their contribution to our tremendous growth since 1917 when LB set up its Home Office here in the Twin Cities.

The integrity of our sales representatives . . . Enfrid Benson, left, San Francisco, Calif., sold more than $1 million of LB life insurance last year. He says, "I try to deserve the confidence that my friends place in me." Mr. Benson is one of nearly 600 LB agents working in 31 States, the District of Columbia and Canada.

The goodwill of Lutherans everywhere . . . LB contributes substantially to benevolences throughout the Lutheran Church. Here 3 students, Edward P. Drzik, Carolyn Lower and Delvin Hutton represent the 128 scholarships made available to high school, college and seminary students last year. Outstanding loans to help build 497 Lutheran Churches amounted to more than $13 million at the end of 1955.

The faith of our policyholders . . . The Glenn Midthun family, San Luis Obispo, Calif.—a 100% LB-protected family—represents nearly a quarter million policyholders who have put their faith in LB for more than $630 million of life insurance. Mark, Linda, Mom and Dad share the security provided by LB insurance.

The spirit of our home office employees . . . Shirley Telschow, right, working here with Marie Rindal and Harvey Skaar, supervisor of the Policy Issue Division, says, "When I came here 6 months ago, I was so surprised how friendly everyone was — just like one big working 'family'. I've found that spirit helps me get my work done better and faster."

```
INSURANCE IN FORCE DEC. 31, 1955
       $633,760,967
```

Our faith in the future of Minneapolis is expressed by our new Home Office building — located in the heart of downtown Minneapolis at 7th Street and 2nd Avenue So.

Lutheran Brotherhood

Living Benefits for Lutherans through Life Insurance

Minnesota School of Business

24 SOUTH SEVENTH STREET

MINNEAPOLIS, MINNESOTA

BEST WISHES.....

to the thousand and one business
firms that have contributed so much
to make Minneapolis a great city.

SINCE 1877.....

the Minnesota School of Business
—through its more than sixty-thousand
graduates — has had the privilege
of supplying business-trained
personnel to these firms.

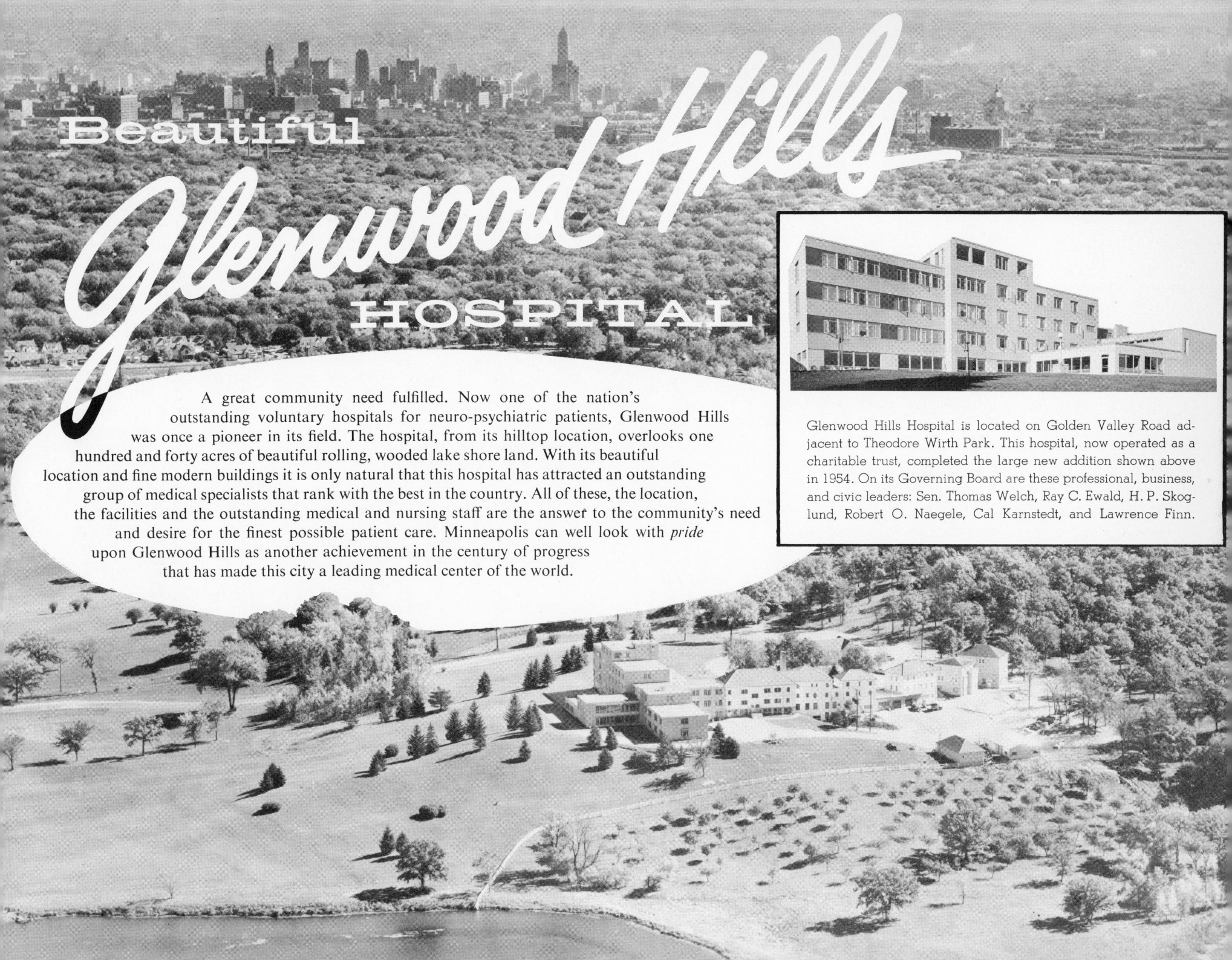

Beautiful *Glenwood Hills* HOSPITAL

A great community need fulfilled. Now one of the nation's outstanding voluntary hospitals for neuro-psychiatric patients, Glenwood Hills was once a pioneer in its field. The hospital, from its hilltop location, overlooks one hundred and forty acres of beautiful rolling, wooded lake shore land. With its beautiful location and fine modern buildings it is only natural that this hospital has attracted an outstanding group of medical specialists that rank with the best in the country. All of these, the location, the facilities and the outstanding medical and nursing staff are the answer to the community's need and desire for the finest possible patient care. Minneapolis can well look with *pride* upon Glenwood Hills as another achievement in the century of progress that has made this city a leading medical center of the world.

Glenwood Hills Hospital is located on Golden Valley Road adjacent to Theodore Wirth Park. This hospital, now operated as a charitable trust, completed the large new addition shown above in 1954. On its Governing Board are these professional, business, and civic leaders: Sen. Thomas Welch, Ray C. Ewald, H. P. Skoglund, Robert O. Naegele, Cal Karnstedt, and Lawrence Finn.

The Public Library

Even before there was a town or city of Minneapolis, the early settlers were interested in forming a library. Many of them came from New England, a bookish region, and brought with them to the raw, new west a love of learning and a respect for literature. In 1850 the St. Anthony Library Association was formed and four years later William W. Wales established his book store.

In 1859 the Young Men's Library Association was formed. Slightly more than $100 was scraped together and sixty-eight books were purchased. The following year the association was incorporated as the Minneapolis Athenaeum and by the time of the Civil War the organization had about 500 volumes.

In 1870 the Athenaeum received an important bequest, real estate in the Washington Avenue district, from Dr. Kirby Spencer, a dentist who had opened an office on Bridge Square in 1863. T. B. Walker, the lumberman who always was interested in the city's cultural life, engineered a change in the Athenaeum's operations in the 1870's. Up to that time it had been a private organization. Walker had the reading room opened to the public.

Herbert Putnam, a young Harvard graduate later to be Librarian of Congress, came out to Minneapolis in 1884 to be librarian of the Athenaeum. A man of vision and leadership, Putnam was quick to recognize the need for a truly public library. He joined with other citizens in pushing plans for a Minneapolis library. In 1885 the state legislature established the Public Library as a tax-supported institution. A library board was set up and T. B. Walker was elected president. In 1886 the board purchased the site at Hennepin Avenue and Tenth Street where the library now stands and a contract was let for construction of a building. The new library was opened December 16, 1889.

"Eager visitors came on foot, in carriages, in horse cars, or if they felt especially venturesome, in the new electric car which had just begun to operate on Hennepin Avenue the week before," according to a description in the fifty-year report of the Public Library.

"Met at the doors by ushers in full dress who showed them into the building," the report continues, "they were greeted by the members of the Library Board and the Librarian. Flowers and soft music formed a pleasant background for the admiration of the guests."

Dr. Putnam, the Athenaeum librarian, became librarian for both institutions. He it was who established the policy, continued down the years, of using Athenaeum funds for the purchase of expensive reference books in restricted fields, Unlike many other libraries of the era, the Minneapolis Public Library opened with a large collection of well-selected books. Dr. Putnam had gone to Europe the year before the opening and had purchased 17,000 volumes. These, with the Athenaeum collection, gave the Public Library a start with more than 30,000 volumes.

In 1892 Dr. Putnam was succeeded by Dr. James K. Hosmer, teacher, librarian and a well-known historian. Under Dr. Hosmer's administration a valuable collection of historical materials was built up.

In the more than half century that the library has served the people of Minneapolis and Hennepin County, probably no person has made a greater contribution to its work than the third librarian, Gratia A. Countryman, who occupied the post from 1904 to 1936.

Miss Countryman had definite ideas of

Inside the Public Library, a teen-age group examines a model of an open-pit mine (right), similar to iron ore operations on the famed Mesabi Range. The younger set (below) listen attentively to a tale of wonder, read to them by a juvenile section librarian.

what a library should be and do. She proceeded to put these ideas into operation.

She once remarked: "How to reach the busy men and women, how to carry wholesome and enjoyable books to the faraway corners of the city, how to enlist the interest of tired factory girls, how to put the working man in touch with the art books relating to his craft and so increase the value of his labor and the dignity of his day's work — these are some of the things which I conceive to be my duty to study . . ."

When Miss Countryman retired she had been so successful in carrying out her ideas for getting the library to the people that the library system included 350 distributing points, including 24 branches, 53 factory and business stations and 15 hospital libraries.

Miss Countryman was succeeded by Carl Vitz who was librarian until 1946. The present librarian, Glenn M. Lewis, succeeded Vitz.

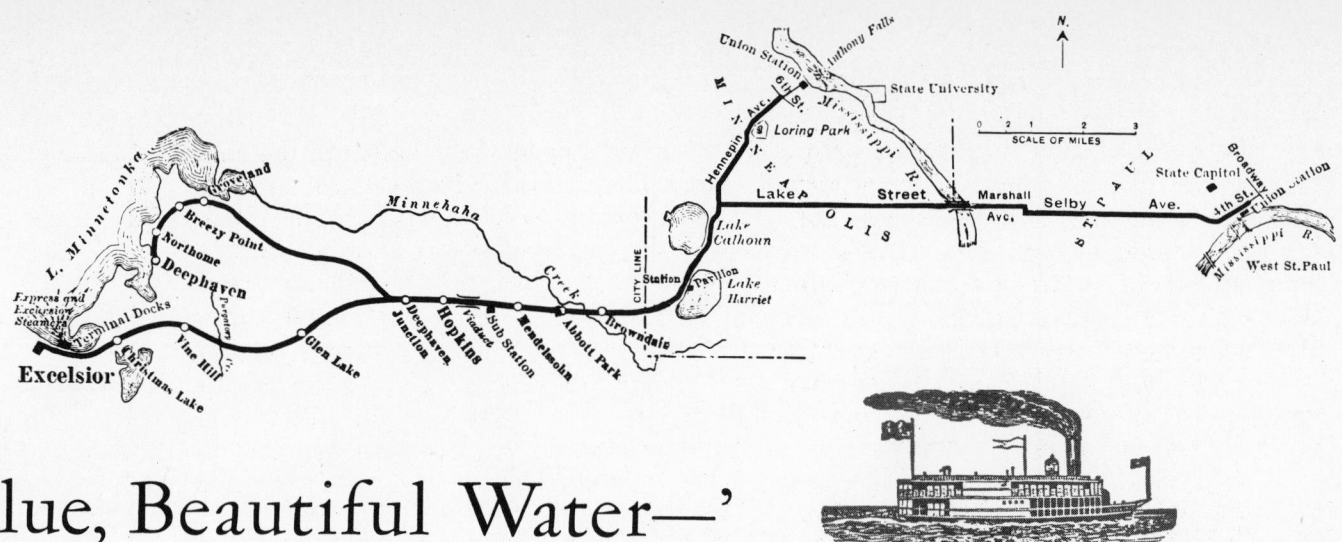

'Big, Blue, Beautiful Water—'

Sometime early in the present century an unknown copywriter for the streetcar company addressed himself to what obviously was a job he could do with enthusiasm—a description of the trolley ride to Lake Minnetonka.

"The most delightful trolley trip you can enjoy in the Twin Cities—or, for that matter, anywhere—" he wrote, "is the one to Excelsior on Lake Minnetonka, and if you have only a few hours to spare, avail yourself of this trip, for it includes a wonderful group of the Twin Cities' most beautiful resorts. Fare from any point in Minneapolis, each way, 25 cents; time, 45 minutes; distance, 18 miles."

This was in the day before the automobile and the paved highway had transformed American life. Carriages were still common on the streets of Minneapolis. A trolley trip to Minnetonka was a thrilling weekend for the whole family.

"Double tracks of 80 pound steel rails," the writer explained, "are laid on a perfectly graded and ballasted right of way, level and straight, except here and there where some long easy curve, planned with the most scientific skill, serves only to turn the scenic page and enhance the pleasure of the trip. Over this smooth, steel roadway the 300-horsepower car speeds along with ease at a mile-a-minute clip.

"Now the western city limits of Minneapolis are passed and the real country is on all sides. Here is a pretty model farm, there a shimmering ridge of upland pasture where the cows stand knee deep in the grass . . .

"The Minnetonka hills now rise on all sides, and the meadows and pastures are narrower and deeper sunk, making a rural landscape to remember . . . Over Purgatory Creek . . . past Vine Hill, and over the meadows again. And then Christmas Lake is seen nestled in among the wooded heights on the left. It is for all the world like one of the lakes of Old England, and its cool woods are deliciously grateful to the eye. No lovelier spot is out-of-doors. And now, before we know it, the car has ascended a steel viaduct, spanning a railroad, and Lake Minnetonka—'The Big, Blue, Beautiful Water'—flashes and gleams before the eye. The car slides smoothly down the incline and stops at the Excelsior Terminal Docks, and the electric ride is over."

Minnetonka had been "discovered" in the early 1820's by two boys on a summer lark from Fort Snelling. One was the drummer boy at the post, Joseph R. Brown, later to be prominent in Minnesota pioneer affairs, and the other was the son of the commanding officer, Colonel Josiah Snelling. But it was another thirty years before the big lake was well known to white men.

Shortly after the Civil War Lake Minnetonka became a resort area. Hotels and boarding houses sprang up around the lake. Summer homes began to appear. By the 1880's big, luxurious hostelries dotted the lake's shores and hundreds of visitors came up from the southern states each year to enjoy Minnesota's summer climate.

In 1878 the Minneapolis, Lyndale, and Lake Calhoun railroad was built from downtown Minneapolis to Thirty-fourth street on the eastern shore of Lake Calhoun, then "way out in the country." In 1881 the line was extended to Excelsior and steam trains were operated until 1887 when the railroad failed and the streetcar company acquired its property. The first electric cars went to Excelsior in 1905. Later the company leased rails from Excelsior to Tonka Bay and to Deephaven from the M & St. L. and the Milwaukee Roads.

As traffic to the lake built up, the company put in a fleet of "streetcar boats." Big Island became a resort park. Three double-end, double deck, paddle ferries, the Minneapolis, St. Paul and Minnetonka, each 108 feet long, 35 feet wide, and with capacity for 1,000 passengers, plied the lake between the Excelsior terminal docks and Big Island.

Referring to Big Island in his glowing description of Lake Minnetonka, the writer for the streetcar company remarked: "Here you can enjoy music by the best bands, as well as many amusement features, revel in the delights of a picnic party, or simply idle away some hours with the glancing, rippling surface of the blue lake all about you. Big Island's exceptional environment, its restful relief from summer heat, its hospitality, and its fine facilities for all who come and go, place it as the favored of Minnesota's amusement resorts. By day, it is a picture; by night, when an electric wand has touched it, it is Fairyland."

Many fine homes were built around the lake. At first, most of these were used simply as summer residences. Minneapolitans commuted, either by the old railroad lines or the electric trolleys. Gradually, over the years, more and more year-around homes were built. With the coming of the automobile and the super highway, the resort atmosphere of Minnetonka faded. Instead of a summer vacation area, Lake Minnetonka became an integral part of the city's all year life.

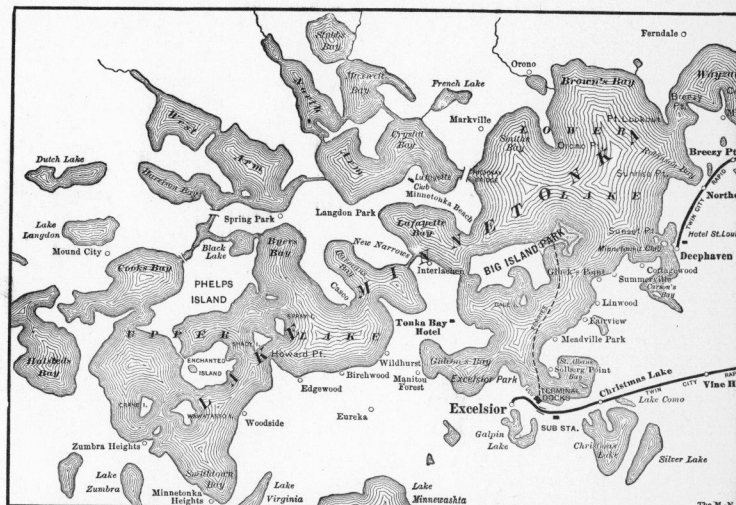

Twin City Rapid Transit Boats docked at Lake Minnetonka in 1912.

A view from the Hotel Keewaydin, 1910.

Health and Hospitals

Today Minneapolis has fifteen major hospitals and many specialized institutions for the care of crippled children, heart disease victims, veterans of the armed services, and others who are physically disabled. The vast group of University of Minnesota hospitals constitutes one of the finest hospital organizations in the world.

Minneapolis' story of medical care goes back to the army surgeons who were stationed at Fort Snelling in pioneer times. One of these, Dr. John Emerson, was the owner of a famous slave, Dred Scott, who married Harriet Robinson, the servant girl of Major Taliaferro.

In the early years after the first settlement there appears to have been some opposition to doctors. Minnesota was being boomed as a health resort. All one had to

do was live here to be healthy. Too many doctors would spoil the story!

Today Minneapolis has a world-wide reputation as a medical center. Heart surgery operations at the University of Minnesota, "deep freeze" surgery, cross circulation operations have written headlines around the world. Patients have been brought here from as far away as Australia. Medical men and students come to Minneapolis from every continent to work and study at the University of Minnesota.

Minneapolis' first hospital, known as Cottage Hospital, was organized in 1870 and opened in 1871 in a rented house on Washington Avenue near Ninth Avenue North. In 1884 its name was changed to St. Barnabas. Minneapolis General Hospital was organized by order of the city council in 1887.

The largest private hospital in Minneapolis is Swedish Hospital (shown on page 216). At upper left is shown the modern entrance to Northwestern Hospital, and a picture at lower left shows the children's section of Abbott Hospital. At left is St. Mary's Hospital and below is a picture of the famous Pamela Schmidt heart operation, previously considered impossible, at the University of Minnesota Heart Hospital. The technique was developed at the University Medical School after years of intensive research.

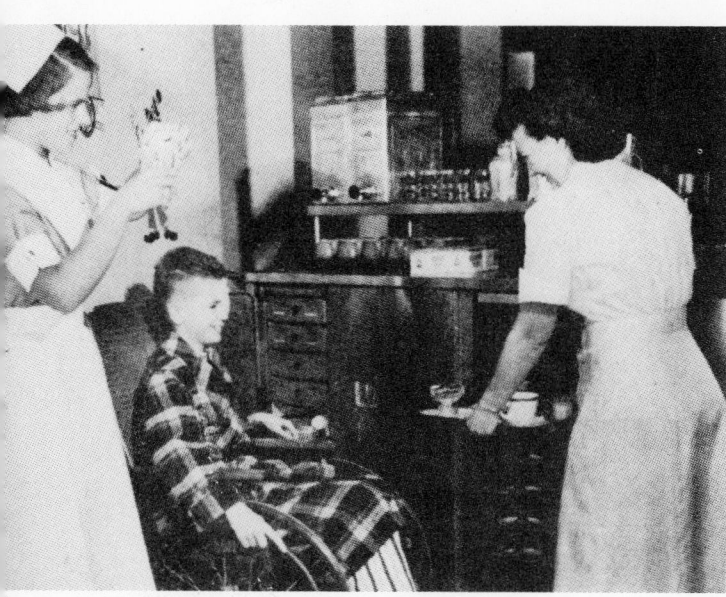

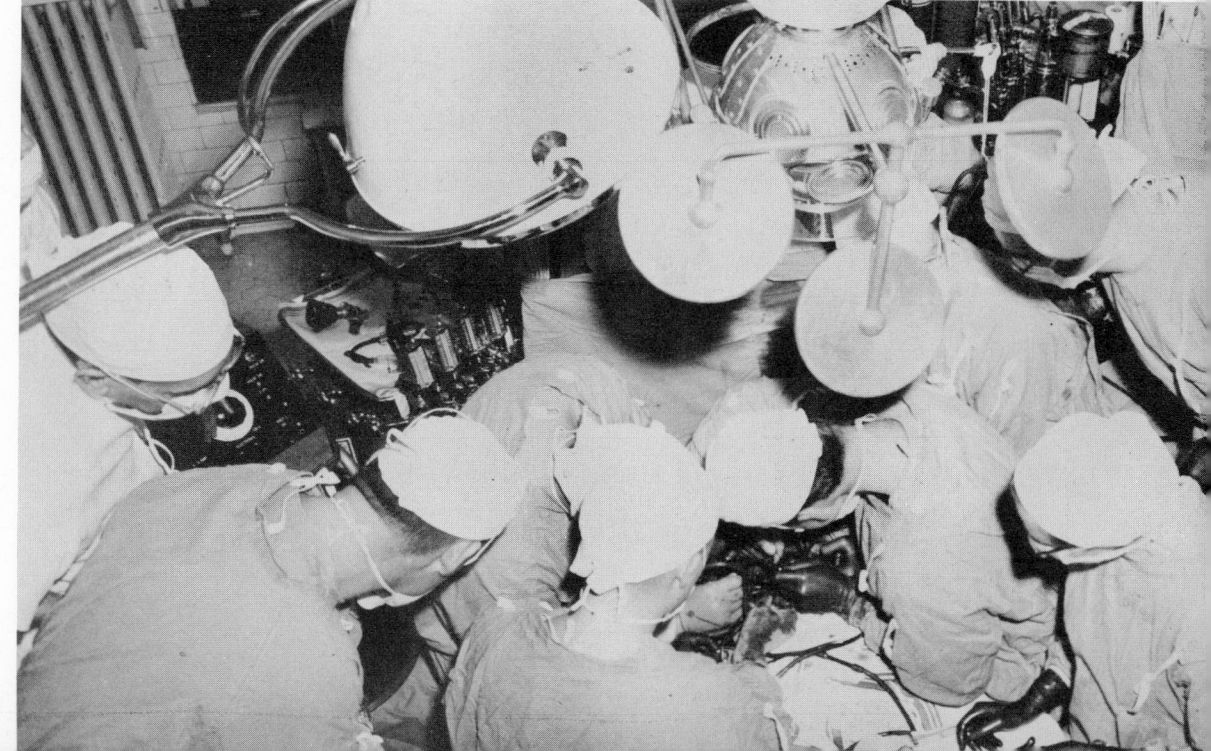

MINNEAPOLIS

CITY OF
NATURAL GAS

Gas holders, a familiar part of the Minneapolis skyline since
the 1870's are a constant reminder of the important role
Modern Gas Service has played in the city's progress.
For industry or home, clean, fast natural gas serves you
best . . . and more economically, too!

MINNEAPOLIS GAS COMPANY

The Police Department

Police Department Baseball Team, 1902

Central Police Station, 1902

On April 14, 1855, St. Anthony elected Benjamin Brown city marshal and the council fixed his salary at $300 a year. He was required to post a $5,000 bond in advance of taking office. As far as can be determined by existing early records this was the first regular police officer in what now is the city of Minneapolis.

In the early days the village had no jail and the marshal had to take prisoners in serious cases cross country to Stillwater for safe keeping until trial. By 1858 a move was on to appoint a night constable in addition to the city marshal, and the following year the marshal's salary was increased $500.

Across the river on the west bank the so-called "town of Minneapolis" appointed a marshal in 1858. C. C. Berkman, A. P. Hoover, Amos Clark, John G. Williams and Lorenzo Coleman were early occupants of the post. It appears from pioneer records that the job was not too popular. It paid only $150 a year.

Shortly after the Civil War, however, the council was ready to add four policemen to the rolls. In 1867 a police force was organized with Henry H. Brackett as chief. There were six patrolmen.

Sawmills and the flour industry were booming in the city, and with the increase in population there was an increase in crime. The city was infested with "tramps." By 1872 the council had a resolution before it calling for one police chief, one captain, one sergeant, and ten patrolmen. The chief's salary was boosted to $1,000 a year. Patrolmen were to receive $60 a month — and it was to be a full-time force, with no jobs allowed "on the side."

220

The squad of police that escorted President Cleveland to the Minneapolis Exposition, Oct. 11th, 1887.

Following the election of John DeLaittre as mayor in 1877 police were ordered to photograph criminals who were arrested. This was the beginning of the police identification bureau. In 1879, Sergeant John West, a veteran of the Union army in the Civil War and later chief of police, commenced drilling the men in an effort to give them the semblance of military discipline.

During the administration of Mayor George A. Pillsbury in 1884 the city attracted a national event, biggest affair of its kind in those days, that inevitably stimulated and increased police work. This was the national encampment of the Grand Army of the Republic, the Union veterans of the Civil War. Mayor Pillsbury found it advisable to add more men to the force. As the veterans came in for their reunion, pick pockets, confidence men and robbers

from all parts of the country flocked to Minneapolis to pick them clean, if they could. The GAR encampment was marked by the killing of two Minneapolis policemen, the first police murders on record.

In 1887 the state legislature passed an act providing for a board of police commissioners. Mayor Albert A. Ames charged that "a few meddlesome fanatics . . . backed by a puritanical majority (of the legislature) . . . succeeded in thwarting the will of the people and depriving the mayor of his control of the police force . . ." Nevertheless and in spite of the mayor's opposition, a board of commissioners, composed of Thomas B. Janney, Michael Hoy and John Baxter, was appointed. The mayor was an ex officio member. The board continued in charge of police affairs until 1890 when it was abolished and control of the

department was returned to the mayor.

Biggest police event of the 1890's was the Harry Hayward murder case which the then mayor, William Henry Eustis, took a personal hand in solving. Eustis was suspicious of Hayward when he came to the mayor's office the morning after the discovery of the body of Catherine Ging, the pretty little dressmaker who had been Hayward's sweetheart. Later, Eustis received a tip from the city's eccentric, recluse lawyer, Levi "Elder" Stewart, which led to Hayward's arrest, trial, and ultimate execution.

By the turn of the century Minneapolis had a police force of more than 200 men. Arrests were averaging better than 5,000 a year. A large mounted patrol had been organized and a police telephone reporting system had been installed.

With the coming of the automobile, the old horse patrol and the horse-drawn "black marias" were superseded. As the city grew and spread out, the needs for a mobile force became more apparent. With the rest of the population, police moved into automobiles and the development of radio brought a more rapid means of communication.

Today, Minneapolis has a police force of 642 men, headed by Chief E. I. "Pat" Walling. It operates 72 automobiles, including 16 uniform squad cars. It has a radio controlled complaint center in the basement of city hall and a teletype system connecting it with Hennepin county law officers and the Minnesota state crime bureau. It is expected that the police teletype system will be extended to include all the suburbs soon.

221

Minneapolis...Home of the 3rd Largest Stamp Company in America

SHOP THE STORE THAT GIVES YOU MORE

GOLD BOND STAMPS

Gold Bond Stamp Company
1629 Hennepin Avenue
Mpls. Minn.

Among the hundreds of leading firms who have grown and prospered in Minneapolis, the progress of the Gold Bond Stamp Company is something of a record.

In 18 short years Gold Bond has grown from an idea to one of the leading companies in a $550,000,000 industry.

Today, Gold Bond is the 3rd largest stamp company in America, with 323 employees, over 60 redemption stores, and a payroll of more than $700,000.

Gold Bond was the first to use the facilities of a major grocery wholesaler to introduce stamps into several hundred stores at once (right here in Minneapolis). This plan with Super Valu stores has led to the wholesale adoption of stamps by leading food chains throughout the country. Today, about 140,000 retailers distribute stamps to more than half the nation's families who save them.

Sandy Saver, the friendly little Gold Bond symbol for thrift, has become a familiar friend in literally millions of American homes. Sandy signifies more than thrift alone, he's symbolic of a progressive company based on sound management, efficient service to its customers, and quality merchandise for consumers.

GOLD BOND STAMP CO.

Established in 1938

ON THE AVENUE: Day or night, December, June, or September, Nicollet Avenue Shops are the show windows of our metropolis. Crowds gather to promenade — to shop — or to join the ever passing parade. Any Minneapolitan will tell you, there is no other avenue like Nicollet.

Congratulations to Minneapolis on her Centennial!

In 1882, when our city was only 26 years old, Gust Lagerquist started in the elevator business, and grew with Minneapolis. The first elevators installed were picturesque hoists, pulled by hand. Today, Lagerquist and Sons, in their 74th year of business, supply the finest of modern elevators of every type, for every purpose.

GUST LAGERQUIST, and Sons
Minneapolis

By night or by day, Minneapolis is a healthy, throbbing, thriving, living city. To and from the heart of downtown over a network of modern highways travel the businessmen, doctors, lawyers, teachers, students, housewives, laboring men and the products they make . . . men, women and children breathing life into the office buildings, banks, factories, clinics, schools, apartments and homes. The only thing which can possibly top natural resources in value to a growing city is the "human resources" . . . the people. And Minneapolis has the finest!

 RAY YAEGER

 SHERM PINKHAM

 TOM CUNNIEN

 MARV HAENZE

 BOB WOLLMAN

 OLLIE MILLER

 LEN HOLZINGER

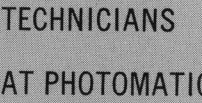 KEITH WHITE

 JOE BARBER

THE

TECHNICIANS

AT PHOTOMATIC

ARE

CAREER

LITHOGRAPHERS

DEDICATED

TO

SERVING

THE

PRINTING

INDUSTRY

 ROG STRAND

 BOB WEISS

 DON ANDERSON

 HAROLD TORVIK

P H O T O M A T I C

1405 CHICAGO AVENUE — MINNEAPOLIS 4

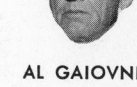 BILL ROMAN

 ELEANOR OLSON

  JARL FECHNER

 HANK BEMLOTT, JR.

 AL GAIOVNIK

 RED MARSHALL

 HANK BEMLOTT, SR.

 LOU THOMAS

 BOB TARALDSON

 BILL NYBERG

 WARREN THOMPSON

 TOM WALKER

 LEN HEDAHL

Every city must plan for its future in its own way. It takes vision, imagination, and dreams — it takes hard work and outstanding ability. The Prudential Insurance Company through the eyes of the artist, George Runge, pictures Minneapolis as it might appear in the future.

The City and The Future

Few men can discern the future. From time to time attempts are made by those who assert special gifts of knowledge or talents for forecasting, but the actuality often outruns the dream. One hundred years ago no one could have foreseen what now rises on the broad riverside acres where John Stevens once planted small grains to prove they could be grown in Minnesota.

So today our vision probably is incommensurate with the future's promise. We can indicate a few possible lines of development, already becoming clear, but the ultimate result a century hence must await fulfillment at the hands of our children and our children's children.

It is obvious that Minneapolis is at the heart of a great new inland empire — an empire of newly utilized materials and newly developed technological skills. The iron and steel industry already has set aside a billion dollars for taconite development in Northern Minnesota, and iron pellets made from formerly worthless low grade ore are now moving in Great Lakes commerce.

In this aerial photo the architectural firm of Thorshov and Cerny shows the contemplated redevelopment of the Minneapolis lower loop area, a major plan that is part of the "New Minneapolis" dream.

The Great Lakes-St. Lawrence seaway, which will carry the cargoes of the oceans to Minnesota's front door, is certain to bring new and unexpected developments. In the immediate future, Minnesota will have a seacoast of its own and, in effect, become a coastal area.

Use of oil, lignite, and uranium from the Dakotas is certain to have an effect on the city in the years to come. We live in an age of chemistry, physics, and electronics. The growth of new industry along these lines is certain to change the contours of the city's life.

Within Minneapolis itself a great new Civic Center is being planned for the old Bridge Square area, the city's birthplace. New superhighways are on the drawing boards. Engineers are discussing ways and means of relieving city traffic which, if carried through, will create many new patterns of life and activity. In the future, deliveries may be made underground. The city may have a vast network of subterranean roadways for more efficient and speedier movement of goods and materials.

Tremendous expansion of the city already is indicated. One of the amazing phenomena of the mid-twentieth century is the rapid spread of people. Within the last decade many Minneapolis suburbs have become small cities themselves. In the next century a vast metropolitan area is certain to spread out from the core center that began to take form a century ago.

In facing forward to the next hundred years Minneapolis will do well to remember its past. A century ago this was a frontier outpost. Today it is one of the great cities of the nation and of the world. Courage, energy, initiative, and belief in themselves characterized the pioneers. They were undaunted men. If in the future we push on to develop, improve and expand our heritage, we must do it in the spirit of the men who built the city. They made Minneapolis' first century a truly great one hundred years.

Acknowledgements

As publishers of this book, "Minneapolis, City of Opportunity," we are indebted to innumerable business firms, organizations, and individuals for their help and cooperation in assembling all the data and material that was necessary to produce it. Our sincere thanks is extended to everyone for this aid, but particularly to the following who gave us special help: The Minneapolis Public Library, The Hennepin County Historic Society, The Minnesota Historical Society, The Minneapolis Institute of Arts, The Minneapolis Star and Tribune, Norton and Peel Photographers and the early files of Hibbard Studios, Don Berg Photographer; The Chamber of Commerce, The Minneapolis Aquatennial Association, Ellertson and Associates, and Photography Inc.

For much of the early photographic records we are especially indebted to Edward A. Bromley and his Minneapolis Album published in 1890, also to the Isaac Atwater History of Minneapolis.

Special commendation is given to the staff of The Brings Press, A. J. Dahl & Co., and Photomatic, Inc., for their untiring efforts to process the book under the pressure of a publication deadline.

We wish to thank the members of the Minneapolis Centennial Committee for their confidence in appointing us the official publishers of this book. During eighty years of book publishing, the preparation of no other book has given us more personal pride and satisfaction than "Minneapolis, City of Opportunity."

T. S. DENISON & COMPANY

Book Publishers since 1876
Minneapolis, Minnesota

T. S. DENISON,
Founder

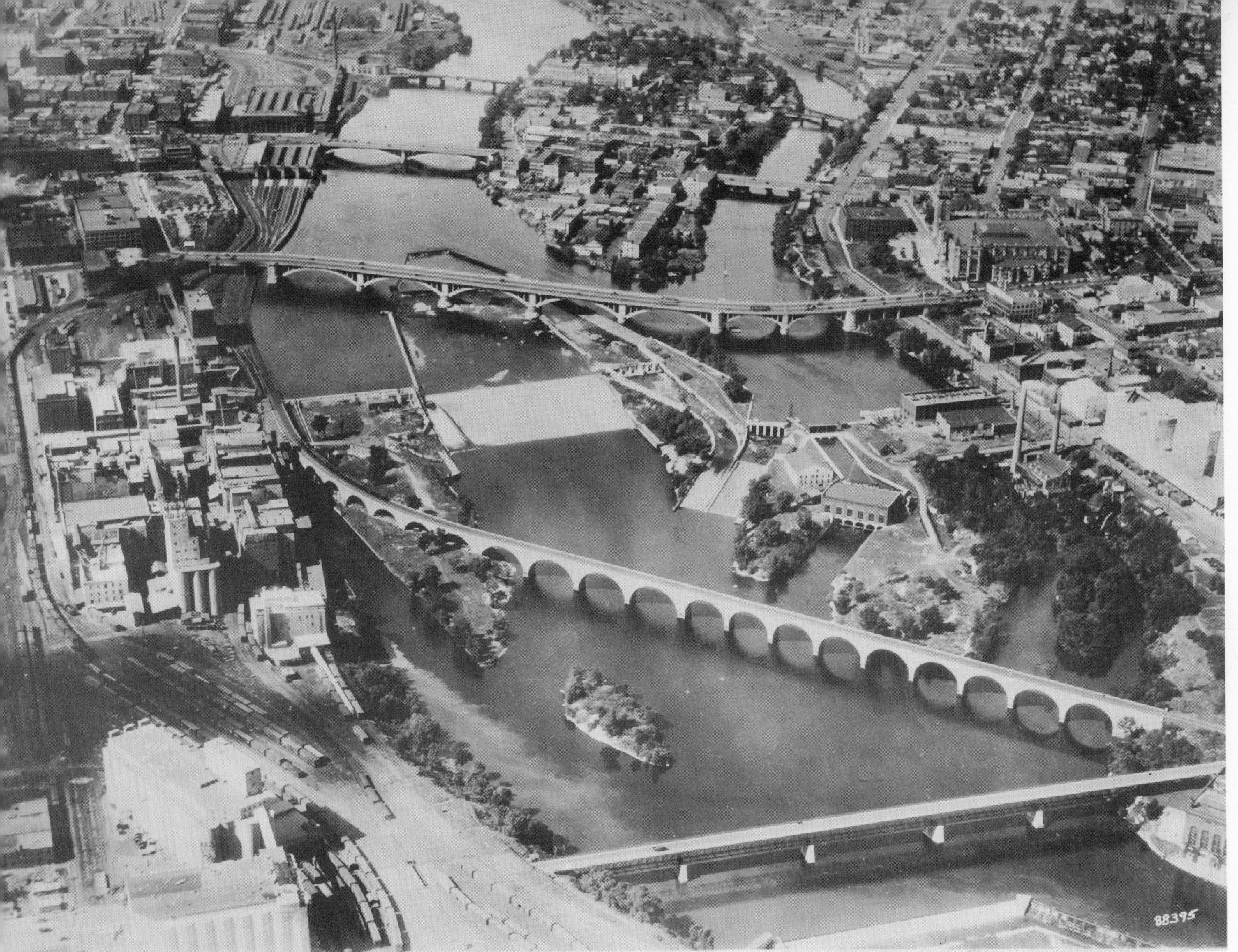

88.395

745

745028

IN GRATEFUL APPRECIATION

You have now completed "the journey" through the official commemorative book about Minneapolis which we have named: "Minneapolis, City of Opportunity." We believe the records of the past century reveal the appropriateness of the title.

The members of our committee wish to thank everyone who encouraged and assisted us in our desire to provide a suitable and lasting remembrance of our city's hundredth birthday. From the many who helped to make this book an actuality, we select the following for special commendation:

The Minneapolis business firms and organizations who sponsored its publication by inserting institutional reviews of their activities.

Mr. Jay Edgerton, whose authorship of the special articles so effectively recreated the atmosphere of early Minneapolis.

Mr. Edmund Kopietz, who, by his sensitive art treatment, has given added significance to the book's contents.

Mr. Lawrence M. Brings, who originally determined the scope of the book and whose faith in its ultimate outcome never diminished.

We hope that this book will help you to better appreciate what an unusual city Minneapolis is, and to understand how wisely our pioneer fathers planned its future — to give us a better community in which to live, to rear and educate our children with high standards, and to earn a livelihood in a thriving city.

As we step off into the second century, we should "take increased devotion" from the example of our forefathers and dedicate ourselves to work diligently for a better and greater Minneapolis of the future.

ERIC G. HOYER,
Mayor of Minneapolis

OTTO SILHA,
President, Mpls. Aquatennial Ass'n.

RAY EWALD,
Chairman

DONALD C. DAYTON

PHILIP PILLSBURY

ARTHUR GLUEK

CLINTON MORRISON

THE MINNEAPOLIS CENTENNIAL COMMITTEE
THE MINNEAPOLIS AQUATENNIAL ASSOCIATION